STONE VOICES

VOICES

Wartime Writings
of Japanese Canadian Issei

Edited by Keibo Oiwa
Foreword by Joy Kogawa

Véhicule Press

MONTRÉAL

Published with the assistance of The Canada Council. Translation from the Japanese funded by the Multiculturalism Programs Branch of Multiculturalism and Citizenship Canada.

Cover art direction and design: JW Stewart
Photograph of cover by Andrew Blanchard
Archival photographs on cover courtesy of National Archives of Canada, and the Japanese-Canadian Cultural Centre of Toronto, and Mrs. Kotoma Kitagawa.
Calligraphy by Kano Futamura.
Typesetting and design: ECW Type & Art.
Printed by Les Editions Marquis Ltée.

CANADIAN CATALOGUING IN PUBLICATION DATA

Main entry under title:

Stone Voices

Included bibliographical references.
ISBN 1-55065-014-9

1. Japanese Canadians — Evacuation and relocation, 1942-1945 — Personal narratives. 2. Japanese Canadians — Biography. I. Oiwa, Keibo.

FC106.J3S86 1991   971'.00495'6   C91-090601-7
F1035.J3S86 1991

Véhicule Press, P.O.B. 125, Place Du Parc Station, Montreal, Quebec H2W 2M9 Distributed in Canada by University of Toronto Press; and in the U.S. by University of Toronto Press (Buffalo, NY), Inland Book Company (New Haven, CT), and Bookslinger Inc. (St. Paul, MN).

Printed in Canada on acid-free paper.

Contents

Foreword

JOY KOGAWA

Within the Canadian patchwork quilt is a bright little square reserved for Japanese Canadians. Interestingly enough, every single thread in that patch, like every other thread in every other human patch, is made of an infinite mix of shadings and colours. Our country, as this book shows, is formed of complex individuals who defy stereotyping.

I devoured these stories in one hungry afternoon of reading. Some of it was painfully familiar. Some of the flavouring tasted strange and felt unsettling. Here were some Issei, professing in their diaries, an identity with a country that was the enemy country of my youth. As a passionately Canadian Nisei, I never did want to believe that Japanese Canadians were anything but totally Canadian in their identity. This was unreasonable. How could I expect people to feel no connection to the land of their birth? As I read, I ranged through discomfort, old sadness, nostalgia, admiration, tenderness, pride, and anger as I was taken back to look again with the help of these additional perspectives, into the secrets and intimacies of my childhood.

There was a time, not too long ago, when, debilitated by Canadian racism, I would have been unable to read this book. Now, my rekindled appetite for stories from my community, told me I was healing. I'm grateful for the lives of Koichiro Miyazaki, Kensuke Kitagawa, Kaoru Ikeda, and Genshichi Takahashi. They enrich our awareness of the human condition and educate our hearts. We are endebted to Keibo Oiwa, whose loving labour has brought these stories into the light of our new post-redress day.

Acknowledgements

This book is a by-product of a larger research project on Japanese-Canadian history which was started by the History Committee of the Japanese Cultural Centre of Montreal in 1982 and is still continuing. I wish to acknowledge the great contribution to this project of the people in the Japanese Canadian community in Montreal who have participated in interviews and volunteered their time and effort. The person who initiated and has been coordinating this collective effort is a remarkable community leader by the name of Rei Nakashima. She drew me into this project. I was in Montreal just finishing up my dissertation on the old Jewish immigrant district in Montreal for Cornell University when I was 'formally' introduced to the Nikkei community which took me in with warmth and patience. For a native Japanese like myself, studying about the Nikkei has at the same time meant learning to become one. I thank Rei for her leadership and friendship. I am also grateful to other members of the committee and volunteers, especially Shigeru Watanabe and Sandra Kawai.

The most important contributors to this book, needless to say, are the Issei writers themselves. I would like to pay homage to Koichiro Miyazaki, Kensuke Kitagawa, and Kaoru Ikeda and thank them for their legacy. It has been one of the most meaningful experiences during my life in Canada that I met Genshichi Takahashi and became his interviewer, pupil, neighbour, and friend. And I wish to acknowledge Mika Takahashi's contribution to her husband's exciting life history of which she is really a co-producer. Ms. Reika Miyazaki, daughter of Koichiro Miyazaki; Mrs. Chisato Tokunaga, daughter of Kaoru Ikeda; and Mrs. Kotoma Kitagawa, Kensuke Kitagawa's wife, have not only been cooperative but enthusiastic about this project. Their participation has added a deep meaning to this book. I was most fortunate to receive assistance from such accomplished writers as Anne Diamond and Thom Richardson. I also wish to thank all of my friends and family members who helped me in one way or another. To name just a few: Rose Aihoshi,

Kano Futamura, Christine Hara, Edward Hillel, Jessie Nishihata, Mari Sato, Merrily Weisbord, and Shulamis Yelin.

My research has been supported by the Multiculturalism program of Multiculturalism and Citizenship Canada, the Secretary of State of Canada, the Social Science and Humanities Research Council of Canada, and the Japanese Canadian Redress Foundation. I thank professors Audrey Kobayashi and Morton Weinfeld of McGill University for arranging the position of post-doctoral researcher at McGill. This book attempts to be a small symbol of my gratitude for my teachers Robert J. Smith of Cornell University and David Rome of the Canadian Jewish Congress Archives who have encouraged me to study the Nikkei. I hope this also symbolizes a beginning for my life as a Nikkei.

Finally, I thank Simon Dardick, my publisher for his commitment and support. There must be a special meaning in the fact that *Stone Voices* is published not in Toronto or Vancouver, but in Montreal, on the periphery of Japanese-Canadian society.

Introduction

1

Japanese Canadians or Nikkei-Kanadajin immigrated from Japan and settled in Canada over one hundred years ago. In Japanese the first generation of immigrants are called Issei (literally "first generation"), their children are Nisei (second generation), their grandchildren are Sansei (third generation) and so forth. The Issei came from Japan and remained in Canada to create a better future for themselves, their families, and descendants.

Nikkei-Canadian history may be divided into two periods, with the outbreak of the Pacific War on December 7, 1941 as the dividing line. The first period is, by and large, the history of the Issei and is "above all, a history of a racial minority struggling to survive in a hostile land."[1] The first Japanese immigrant is believed to have arrived in Canada in 1877. Before the end of the nineteenth century, Canadian passenger ships regularly plied the trans-Pacific route, bringing nearly 5,000 Japanese immigrant workers to Canada.

In the first, pre-war period, nearly 95% of the Nikkei population was concentrated in a small area of southwest British Columbia, no more than a dot in the corner of the huge map of Canada. Immigrant workers from Japan participated in the early settlement of the young province. They soon became an essential part of the fishing, mining and lumber industries.

The early Nikkei settlements, which consisted almost exclusively of male migrant workers, were temporary and unstable in nature. In the second decade of this century, as "picture brides"[2] began arriving en masse from Japan to join their prospective husbands, the Nikkei aggregation grew to form permanent communities.[3]

Constrained by racial discrimination, both formal and informal, the Nikkei-Canadian community constituted a small, largely self-contained society within British Columbia. Not unlike those of Chinese and Hindu origin, Japanese Canadians were deeply resented by white society. Throughout this first half of Japanese-Canadian history, the British

Issei women in Canada, 1934.

Columbia government made great efforts to curtail both the numbers and the civil liberties of the Nikkei population. Most whites found it simply unacceptable that Asians should stand as their equals. The animosity reached a climax in 1907 when as many as 5,000 whites went on a rampage in the Japanese and Chinese quarters of Vancouver.

From that time until the end of the Second World War, there was no significant decrease in popular anti-Japanese sentiment — the difference between Nihonjin, or Japanese, and Nikkei-Kanadajin, or Japanese Canadian, was considered inconsequential. An anti-Japanese platform would always help local politicians get elected. Sanctions against the militaristic government of Japan and discriminatory laws against Canadian citizens of Japanese descent were never logically differentiated. This situation became more exaggerated as the political relationship between Japan and North America became increasingly tense, until finally Japan's attack on Pearl Harbour ignited the war in the Pacific.

Vancouver was the heart of Japanese Canada. In the pre-war years, the city was home to nearly 40% of the Japanese Canadian population, of which the great majority was concentrated in the small area along Powell Street, forming an ethnic enclave known as Nihon-machi (Japantown), or "Little Tokyo." Political, economic, educational and religious institutions, and organizations with almost exclusively ethnic clientele thrived, along with a great number of commercial establishments. The community boasted Japanese bath houses, Japanese-language newspapers, Japanese language school, a judo club, Buddhist and Christian churches, gambling parlours, restaurants, and stores offering an assortment of Japanese foods. Smaller communities were also formed throughout the province: Steveston and other fishing villages, sawmill towns along the Pacific coast and on Vancouver Island, and agricultural communities in the Fraser and Okanagan valleys.

According to the census data, in 1941 the entire Nikkei population in Canada was 23,149. Of this figure, the ratio between Issei and Nisei generations was about two to three.[4] One source informs us that in 1934, those over twenty years-of-age constituted approximately 12% of the Nikkei population, and 36.5% in 1941. Their birth rate peaked in 1929.[5] Thus, the prewar years saw only the early stage of the Nisei's coming of age, which really began on a full-scale during the wartime and post-war years.

•   •   •

The second period of Japanese-Canadian history covers the years during and after the Pacific war. The setting shifts to include all of Canada as the Nikkei became scattered along the 5,000-km.-long Canada-United States border.

Immediately after the Pearl Harbour attack on December 7, 1941, all persons of Japanese descent, even Canadian citizens, were identified as "enemy aliens." Within hours, about forty Japanese nationals suspected of being "dangerous elements" were detained. Other measures quickly followed, all in the name of security. The entire fleet of about 1,200 Nikkei-Canadian fishing vessels was impounded. Automobiles, radios and cameras were confiscated and a night-time curfew was imposed. All Japanese Canadians were required to register with the newly-established British Columbia Security Commission, in charge of all matters pertaining to the Nikkei, and were required to carry special identification. By the end of February 1942, the government decreed that all Nikkei residing in the "protected area" of coastal British Columbia, that is about 21,000, or more than 90% of the entire Nikkei population in Canada, were to be removed. In the prevailing climate of hysteria, the War Measures Act was enacted and used to justify racism.

By the end of October the same year, the Nikkei throughout coastal British Columbia were thoroughly uprooted. Those living outside the Vancouver area were first herded into the Hastings Park Exhibition Grounds, which was converted into a temporary transit centre. After weeks or months of humiliating imprisonment in buildings which had previously housed livestock, they were sent to the so-called "relocation camps" in the interior of British Columbia and elsewhere. The largest group, about 12,000, had been installed in old ghost towns in the mountains, or in shanty towns hastily built by Nikkei work crews. Of this group, the largest number of nearly 5,000 were concentrated in the Slocan Valley, British Columbia, forming separate camps at Slocan City, Bay Farm, Popoff, Lemon Creek, and in other locations. [6] About 4,000 in family units had been sent to the Prairie Provinces where they worked on the sugar beet farms under harsh conditions. It must not be overlooked that approximately 700 men were detained in prisoner-of-war camps in Ontario, first at Petawawa, then Angler. Most of those imprisoned were accused of disobeying and resisting the authorities, or planning to do so, and were called *ganbari-ya* or die-hards, sometimes with admiration, sometimes in mockery, by fellow Japanese Canadians.

While a similar process was going on in the United States, one may

National Archives of Canada

argue that, in some ways, the persecution of the Nikkei Canadians was even harsher than that of the Nikkei Americans. By quickly liquidating the confiscated homes, businesses, farms and other personal possessions without consultation with the Nikkei owners, and by prohibiting them from returning to the coastal area until 1949, the federal government led by Mackenzie King allowed the destruction of pre-war Nikkei society. It is evident that even after the war, anti-Japanese racists in British Columbia did not give up their dream of getting rid of all "Japs,"not only in British Columbia but across Canada.

Toward the end of the war, while 120,000 Japanese Americans had been permitted to return to their homes on the West Coast, the great majority of Japanese Canadians still remaining in the interior camps were given a choice: move themselves east of the Rockies, or sign papers renouncing their Canadian citizenship and agree to be "repatriated,"(but in fact deported), to Japan. As public support grew for their right to stay in Canada, the government's deportation policy was finally cancelled but not before approximately 4,000 people were shipped to Japan. Under the order to "relocate" again, and this time disperse themselves throughout Canada, many Nikkei chose to try their luck in Eastern Canada.[7]

In the 1950s some Nikkei began to move back to the coastal area of British Columbia where discrimination, both formal and informal, was supposed to have ceased, and formed the basis of today's thriving community. A considerable number of those who had been deported to post-war Japan only to find the country devastated by the war, began to return to Canada. They were referred to as *kika* or returnees. To add to these demographical changes, a trickle of new Japanese immigrants began to arrive in the 1960s, as Canada reopened its doors.

In 1977, Nikkei communities scattered throughout Canada celebrated the 100th year of Japanese-Canadian history. It was an occasion with much symbolic significance, for until that time Japanese Canadians, by and large, had kept a low profile, almost as if deliberately avoiding attention from the larger society. The 100th anniversary was probably their first major attempt since World War II to reintroduce themselves to mainstream Canadian society and to seek their place as an ethnic minority within the rapidly-changing Canadian mosaic. At that time, Canada had begun to embrace new national principles of pluralism and multiculturalism, and ethnic and racial minorities were actively engaged in tackling discrimination and asserting their rights.

According to a recent demographic study, the Japanese-Canadian population in 1986 was 54,505[8]. Of this number, those who immigrated from Japan before 1950 represent only 3.2%.[9] The Issei population is rapidly disappearing and their children, the Nisei, are growing old. The memory of the wartime experience wedged into Nikkei history is fading.

On September 22, 1988, the Canadian government announced the Redress Settlement for the wartime mistreatment of Japanese Canadians. This historic agreement was signed with the National Association of Japanese Canadians (NAJC), the nucleus of the national movements for redress. The agreement included the government's formal apology to Japanese Canadians and symbolic payments for surviving individuals and communities. For the members of the NAJC and supporters of the redress movement, the settlement was a great achievement in the Canadian people's struggle for justice and human rights, and an inspiration for native people and Canada's ethnic minorities. With this in mind, one could postulate that Nikkei Canadians are experiencing a turning point in their history. The third period of Nikkei history, following the prewar and postwar periods, has now begun.

2

This book is about the Issei, their prewar and wartime experiences. It is a selection of some of the finest written accounts by Issei themselves, translated for the first time from Japanese into English.

It is curious that most of the writings on Japanese-Canadian history have characteristically been "a history in passive voice" — a history in which a people, instead of being the main actors and thinkers, were the objects of other people's action and thought. It is as if they had never played a creative role in their own history, and their history was simply created by others. In the prewar, wartime and immediate postwar years, Japanese Canadians almost always appear in history as victims of discrimination, uprooting, incarceration and dispersal. It is as if the history of the persecuted could be reduced to what their persecutors did. We rarely encounter accounts of what the persecuted themselves felt, thought, wished to do, and actually did or failed to do; what meanings they attached to their thoughts and actions. There seems to be a blank space in Japanese-Canadian history.

It is not that there has been no explanation about this void; it has, for instance, been identified as "silence." The Nikkei in North America have often been characterized as "reticent and quiet" folk who keep silent about their own wartime experience even with their own children. While the "quiet Nikkei" has become an ethnic stereotype, few serious attempts have been made to reach the depths of this socio-psychological phenomenon. The Japanese-Canadian poet, Joy Kogawa, opened her novel *Obasan*, a novel based on her own wartime experience, with an unforgettable passage about "silence." To quote just part of it:

There is a silence that cannot speak.
There is a silence that will not speak.
Beneath the grass the speaking dreams and beneath the dreams
   is a sensate sea.

The speech that frees comes forth from that amniotic deep.

. . . . .

If I could follow the stream down and down to the hidden voice, would I come at last to the freeing world? I ask the night sky but the silence is steadfast. There is no reply.[10]

Kogawa was actively involved in the redress movement in the 1980s which sought to let Japanese Canadians face their own past. Their unwillingness to remember, their fear of talking, and their tendency to blame the victims (themselves), and even to justify injustice as a "blessing in disguise," constituted a large obstacle. The first thing that needed to be addressed was their own silence. The movement and the resulting success of the redress settlement have no doubt been a great encouragement and inspiration for many Japanese Canadians who had been unwilling to begin dealing with their past experiences. I hope that this book will be an instrument for the continuing process of psychological healing.

Although I do not wish to make the error of "blaming the victim," it is necessary to mention what can be called "self-censorship" among Japanese Canadians. This "self-censorship" has contributed to the "silence" and the blank space in their history. I believe it was just after the redress settlement in 1988 when small segments of recollections by some Issei appeared in a local community newspaper. One Nisei man approached the editor to express his anxiety about how some Issei dared to say in the article that they had felt excited over Japan's military advance in the early part of the Pacific war, and that they had felt sad at the news of Japan's surrender. "Since when are we allowed to say something like that?" he asked. For him, the statements of these Issei community members were an embarrassment, especially with public attention focusing on the community after the redress settlement.

As in any ethnic community, there have always been embarrassing things in the Nikkei community that the majority feel should be kept hidden from outsiders. Prewar Japanese-Canadian society seems to have been rich in such sensitive areas. Brothels and gambling parlours were two indispensable institutions of the Vancouver community. Etsuji Morii, the *éminence grise* of the business and gambling world of Powell Street was so powerful in the prewar community that the British Columbia Security Commission appointed him as the main liaison person with the Japanese community at the beginning of the war, hoping to make use of his influence.[11] There were also strong syndicalist and leftist currents, parts of which would join the Canadian Communist Party. In the minds of many, these were, and still are, embarrassing.

During, and just after the war, the main source of embarrassment for many Japanese Canadians were the *ganbari-ya*, those who refused to comply with government orders. Many of the most outspoken *ganbari-ya* were interned in POW camps situated in Ontario. However, in every interior camp and settlement there were those who shared the *ganbari-ya* sentiment out of resentment towards Canada for what it did to them, or attachment to their native country, Japan. Between so-called pro-Japan and pro-democracy groups conflicts were common although not as severe as among Nikkei in the United States or in Brazil. A good many people, especially Issei, who could not completely give up the hope that Japan would be victorious, felt deeply shamed at the end of the war.

It is a common phenomenon to feel embarrassment or even shame about the past, whether one's own or someone else's, and also about the past as it is embodied in parents and grandparents. But this seems to be more intense among Japanese Canadians. On many occasions I have heard Nikkei talk of their own and their children's embarrassment about being "Japanese," before, during and just after the war. Young people would often feel self-conscious about their Issei parents, with their poor English, their Japanese customs, rituals, and manners brought from the old country. As Joy Kogawa recalls, children would wish they had been born as a *hakujin*, or white person.[13] It is not difficult to imagine that such a sentiment, akin to self-hatred, was a product of the many years of racial prejudice and discrimination that the Nikkei had to experience in Canadian society. At the same time, it is hard to overestimate the particular importance of their war experience in shaping their psycho-sociological configuration.

Stone Voices focuses on the period during the Pacific War as it was experienced by the Issei. I believe the entire Nikkei history in Canada continues to revolve around the wartime experience of uprooting, incarceration, and dispersal. This book is an attempt to touch the core of that experience.

The political settlement of redress no doubt has lifted to some extent the heavy cloud of reticence and self-censorship among the Nikkei. To restore the lost pages of history is not an easy task. Language has been a great problem, especially for the Japanese-speaking Issei. After the war, when assimilation and dispersal became the slogan of the day, the Japanese language went "underground" so to speak. The linguistic gap between generations began to widen. It became difficult to distinguish what the Issei did not want to talk about from what they wanted to but could not express. It is also true that the linguistic barrier between generations often goes with cultural and social discontinuity. As Kogawa says, "There is a silence that cannot speak."

•   •   •

Several years ago, I began to try to penetrate that silence which is presumed to surround the Issei. Instead of unwillingness to talk, I discovered shyness, humility, and a sense of resignation. The many individuals I spoke to maintained that they did not have anything interesting and exciting to say, that they were just simple and ordinary folk. They were very sorry to be so boring and they probably mean it too. When I insisted that I wanted to hear 'simple and ordinary' stories about their lives, they slowly begin to talk. I realized then that the slowness to speak may have been due to a pessimistic feeling that they would not be understood. *Hakujin*, whites, would not understand, not only because of the language barrier, but also because in the minds of the Issei they belonged to a different "class." The younger generation of Japanese Canadians would not understand either, because of the linguistic, cultural, and social gap.

Finally, there is a sentiment that they, the Nikkei, cannot be understood by the Japanese in Japan; although there has been a general lack of concern in Japan for those who left the country for another. The other side of this sentiment is a tendency to want to defend the Japanese. The Issei would say, "Shikata ga nai" (It cannot be helped), adding that "Japan has different traditions and customs." I am familiar with this saying because it is often used by Japanese politicians to justify their chauvinistic ideas. The Issei seem extremely patient, not only with the native Japanese, but also with the Canadians who surround them. They do not blame others for not being able to understand them. I believe they do not feel frustrated or bitter against those who fail to understand. If they did so, then they have somehow managed to outgrow that state of mind.

These writings by Issei Japanese Canadians are far from being simple and ordinary, and I think it is not mere coincidence that they are diaries and memoirs which were written with almost no intention of being read by more than a few individuals. In spite of the private nature of these writings, they are written in clear yet passionate language, as if the authors were continuously moved by the desire to communicate. We can only guess whom they were subconsciously addressing.

•   •   •

Koichiro Miyazaki's (1902-1978) diary and letters were mostly written during his internment days, 1942-44, at Petawawa and Angler POW camps in Ontario. The diary and other manuscripts were found in the basement of a former pupil nearly ten years after his death. I am quite certain that much of it has remained unread before and after his death although his wish to publish parts of the manuscripts seems evident.

The letters of Kensuke Kitagawa (1895-1974) were sent from Angler prison camp to his wife. The original letters were lost but fortunately his wife had copied into a notebook many of the letters she received during the first half of the Pacific War.

Kaoru Ikeda (1875-1946) kept her diary, selections of which are included here, during her stay from 1942-45 at Slocan "relocation camp" in the interior of British Columbia. Her "Slocan Diary" has been retained as an heirloom for more than forty years by her daughter who, I believe, had been its sole reader.

Genshichi Takahashi (1904-) wrote the first version of his memoir "Footsteps" in 1982. Only the sections covering his prewar and wartime years are included in *Stone Voices*. The memoir was written at his cousin's insistence and as soon as it was completed, the neatly handwritten manuscript was sent from Montreal, where the author lives, to the cousin in Vancouver. From that time, it remained inside the family Buddhist altar, probably without ever being read by anyone except the cousin himself, until I had the good fortune to be given permission to read it. It took a great deal of effort and much time to persuade the author to show me the manuscript and then to let me edit and translate it for publication. Even today, he continues to shake his head, saying, "You are wasting time and energy on my useless stuff." He is a typical Issei who continually tells me that I could never imagine what it was like in the old days. Yet he has turned out to be one of my best guides in my ongoing fieldwork among Japanese Canadians.

To me, these are remarkable and unusual individuals. Critics may complain that these Japanese Canadians are not representative and are too marginal. They are certainly marginal if that means they do not easily fit the Japanese-Canadian stereotype. Koichiro Miyazaki was a self-proclaimed right-winger, an heir of the Japanese tradition of romanticism and patriotism, who at the beginning of the war chose to become a "beautiful prisoner" rather than fight against his native country and his own kin. He was one of the intellectual Issei who played a leading role in prison life at the internment camps. Kensuke Kitagawa, also in the same prison camp, sustained his *ganbari* spirit with his new-found religious conviction and would go so far as to remain in the *ganbari-ya* group even after the war.

Kaoru Ikeda, one of few Nikkei women with a high level of education and literacy, was married to Arichika Ikeda, an explorer-entrepreneur, and a pioneer of Nikkei history. It is remarkable to find a woman writer in prewar Japanese-Canadian society where women were culturally and socially marginalized.

Genshichi Takahashi is a self-proclaimed socialist who was once a leader of the most radical faction of the Japanese-Canadian union movement, too radical for the charismatic union leader and journalist, Etsu Suzuki, to tolerate him in the union. He was a man who, at the beginning of the war, anticipated Japan's eventual defeat and even expressed this belief openly.

Coming from the pens of these individuals, these diaries, memoirs, letters, and poems capture the inner core of the experience shared by a great many "ordinary" Nikkei: they are Japanese-Canadian stories *par excellence*. Although these writers may not have been typical Japanese Canadians, their idiosyncrasies did not turn them into alienated loners. Despite their differences, they were integrated members of their community, with many friends and family grouped around them. One may even say that their uniqueness was rooted in the day-to-day experience of ordinary Japanese Canadians.

•   •   •

It is my opinion that the pluralistic nature of Nikkei culture has been largely invisible since assimilationism became the dominant ideology after the war. The prewar world of the Issei was far from monolithic; the assortment of subcultures brought from Japan was further diversified by the difference in people's attitudes toward their new social environment. There was a colourful mosaic of ideologies: nationalism, patriotism, Buddhism, Shinto tradition, Christianity, democracy, Marxism, labour unionism, and often a "confused *melange* of several of these."[14] As anthropologist Clifford Geertz has said of ideology: "It is in country unfamiliar emotionally or topographically that one needs poems and roadmaps. So too with ideology."[15]

The labour union movement in which Mr. Takahashi found himself involved as a leftwinger was by no means a minor episode in Nikkei history. Its more than 1,000 members and supporters formed a powerful political block against the Nikkei establishment gathered around the Nihonjin-kai, the Japanese Association in Vancouver. The movement of *ganbari* or disobedience, in which Koichiro Miyazaki and Kensuke Kitagawa participated, was also a major event in Japanese-Canadian history. There has been a tendency in and around the Nikkei community to underestimate or underplay wartime resistance, which took many different forms. Those who ended up in the Petawawa and Angler POW camps amounted to 700, a significant portion of the Nikkei adult male population of the time. The reader will find that many of the sentiments underlying Miyazaki's resistance were akin to Kaoru Ikeda's. Though her voice is more subdued, Ikeda too expresses the ideological conflicts going on within herself: on the one hand, her sense of Japanese nationalism grew along with the harsh treatment by the host society, but on the other hand, she was increasingly sympathetic to the desire of Canadian-born Nisei, her children's generation, to be fully accepted as Canadian. This was no doubt one of the most common ideological problems troubling the minds of the Issei. In the Kitagawa letters, the reader will find how one Issei searched for a solution to the problem by absorbing himself in religious training. Perhaps *Stone Voices* will draw more attention to what has been considered marginal in Japanese-Canadian history and reveal the many different shades within this minority culture.

The descriptions of everyday affairs in these wartime writings is also of anthropological interest. The Ikeda diary, in particular, offers a rare picture of daily life in a relocation camp seen from a woman's point of view. It demonstrates how the women, with their networks of mutual help, coped with the unfamiliar and often harsh environment, so that life became not only tolerable but meaningful and even enjoyable. With the shortage of desirable Japanese foodstuffs, they were most resourceful in cultivating gardens, gathering berries and mushrooms, and inventing ways of preservation as well as new recipes to substitute for traditional dishes. Besides taking care of food, they grew flowers which they often exchanged as gifts, organized classes to learn useful skills, and joined religious, recreational or artistic clubs like the *haiku* poetry group in which Kaoru Ikeda participated. They continued observing both traditional and Western festivals and rites of passage, and inventing substitute ornaments for the children. It was a highly creative period. If we wish to speak about "Nikkei culture," here is a moment in which it was being forged.

The anthropologist Barbara Myerhoff once characterized our species as *Homo narrans*, humankind as storyteller, implying that culture is the 'story' we tell about ourselves.[16] In this sense of the term, this book is a collection of Issei stories, and is about what we may call Japanese-Canadian culture.

Let us now listen to the voices that have been for most of us nothing but steadfast silence.

N O T E S

1. Yuji Ichioka, *The Issei: The World of the First Generation Japanese Immigrants, 1885-1924* (New York: The Free Press, 1988).

2. Tomoko Makabe, *Shashinkon no Tsumatachi* (Tokyo: Mirai-sha, 1983). "Picture brides" refers to a method whereby the traditional *miai*, or system of arranged marriages, was replaced by an exchange of photographs. Many picture brides came to Canada to get married without having met their husbands.

3. Ken Adachi, *The Enemy That Never Was: A History of the Japanese Canadians* (Toronto: McClelland and Stewart, 1976). In 1908, after whites rioted in Asian sections of Vancouver in September, 1907, the Canadian and Japanese governments came to an agreement which stipulated that future Japanese immigration would be strictly controlled. This agreement is often referred to as the Hayashi-Lemieux "gentleman's agreement."

4. Ibid., 414.

5. Mitsuru Shinpo, *Kanada Nihonjin Imin Monogatari* (Tokyo: Tsukiji-shokan, 1986).

6. Canada, British Columbia Security Commission, *Removal of Japanese from Protected Area*, Vancouver, 31 October 1942 as cited in Ken Adachi, op cit, 415.

7. Canada. Department of Labour, *The Re-establishment of Japanese in Canada 1944-1946*, Ottawa, 1947; *Report of the Department of Labour*, annual reports for fiscal years ending 31 March 1949, as cited in Ken Adachi, op cit, 416. By 31 March 1949 there were 5,650 Japanese Canadians in the Prairie Provinces and 9,100 in Ontario and Quebec. The Japanese Canadian population in these regions were only 664 and 159 respectively on 1 January 1942.

8. Audrey Kobayashi, *A Demographic Profile of Japanese Canadians and Social Implications for the Future* (Ottawa: Secretary of State, 1989), 23.

9. Ibid., 57.

10. Joy Kogawa, *Obasan* (Toronto: Lester and Orpen Dennys, 1981).

11. Ken Adachi, *The Enemy That Never Was*, 192, 237.

12. Joy Kogawa, *Obasan*, 109 and Ken Adachi, *The Enemy That Never Was*, 343.

13. Joy Kogawa, "Odoroki, Warai, Ai," *Nikkei Kanadajin* edited by Shin'ichi Tsuji (Tokyo: Shobun-sha, 1990).

14. Clifford Geertz, *The Interpretation of Cultures* (New York: Basic Books, 1973), 221.

15. Ibid., 218.

16. Barbara Myerhoff, *Number Our Days* (New York: Simon and Schuster, 1980), xv.

The Story of a Diehard

Koichiro Miyazaki

Britain, U.S. Smash at Japan on 6000-Mile Front

The Vancouver Sun

Only Evening Newspaper Owned, Controlled and Operated by Vancouver People

VANCOUVER, BRITISH COLUMBIA, MONDAY, DECEMBER 8, 1941 — Price 3 Cents

U.S.-Jap War Declared in 33 Minutes

'Day That Will Live in Infamy,' Says Roosevelt; 'We Will Triumph, So Help Us, God'

Canada In War on Pacific

Declaration Made At Ottawa Sunday

Japs Invade Malaya and Hong Kong; Siam Quits

City Men Called to Arms

Terrific Air Raids on U.S. Air Bases In Philippines; Manila Attacked 'With Fiendish Accuracy'

City Rapidly Shifts Onto War Footing

'Within the Hour'

Britain Declares War Against Japan

(EDITORIAL)

Citizens, Be Calm!

BULLETIN

Dorothy Thompson

Bruce Hutchison

Hart Offers Tories Four

One Cabinet Job Delays Coalition

Japanese Hit U.S. Oil Dump At Manila Base

Naval Battle Off Hawaii

War Savings Chief Returns from East

B.C. Defenses 'Adequate to Meet Any Probable Attack'

The day after the attack on Pearl Harbour. Front page
of The Vancouver Sun, Monday, December 8, 1941.

Courtesy of The Vancouver Sun

The Story of a Diehard

KOICHIRO MIYAZAKI

Editor's Introduction

Koichiro Miyazaki was born in 1902 in Chiba Prefecture, Japan. After working as a school teacher in Japan he came to Vancouver when he was twenty-seven, accompanied by his wife Yoshiko, who had also been a school teacher. There he worked both as the principal of a Japanese language school in the Fairview district of Vancouver and as a journalist for a Nikkei newspaper. Miyazaki and his wife lived in the school where they taught. After the Pacific War broke out Miyazaki became upset with the Canadian government's policy of removing Japanese Canadians from the West Coast and with some of the Nikkei leaders who were cooperating with the government. He chose to disobey the government's directives and in March 1942 he was arrested and sent to an internment camp as one of the *ganbari-ya*, or die-hards. For the next two-and-a-half years he was a prisoner in the Petawawa and Angler camps in Ontario. These internment camps once held more than seven hundred Issei and Nisei men, including about forty Issei who were arrested immediately after the Japanese attack on Pearl Harbour. Also rounded up were those who were considered suspicious or who openly resisted the government.

In 1944, Miyazaki reluctantly made an appeal to be released from Angler camp in order to join his wife who had fallen seriously ill in Montreal. Finding work as a labourer he rebuilt his life from scratch and remained in Montreal until his death in 1978. He was an active member of the local Nikkei community. Two years before his death, the staff of the Japanese pictorial magazine *Mainichi Gurafu* was in Montreal reporting

The marriage of Koichiro and Yoshiko Miyazaki in Japan.
A formal portrait taken in front of a shrine.

Courtesy of Reika Miyazaki

on the Olympic Games. They included several pages of photographs and articles about Miyazaki. In one of the photographs, Miyazaki is sitting on a bed in a small room tenderly holding a small box wrapped in white cloth containing his wife's ashes. Other photographs show a tower of books by nationalist author Yukio Mishima; Miyazaki working busily on a manuscript holding a cigarette in one hand; piles of his manuscripts all over the room.

In 1974 Miyazaki produced about one hundred mimeographed copies of a hand-written manuscript on the history of Japanese Canadians. Except for this one book, his large body of writings, in the form of diaries, letters, and notes, along with his collection of documents and books, remained dormant in the basement of a friend's house for nearly ten years. What follows is only an edited portion of the manuscripts he left behind.

The first part is a memoir describing the days following the attack on Pearl Harbour in December 1941, and then the events leading to his arrest in March 1942. The reader will find an interesting account of his reaction to the Pearl Harbour attack and to the following chaos that descended upon the Vancouver Nikkei community. As an intellectual he was knowledgeable about the precarious circumstances surrounding Japanese Canadians. He especially had a sympathetic understanding of the situation of Canadian-born Nisei, including his students and his own child. His position on the crisis quickly emerged — he chose to become a "beautiful prisoner" rather than take up arms against his native country. As a devout Japanese nationalist he felt his arrest was imminent when many Japanese school principals began to be arrested. From that time on he regarded himself as an actor in a drama; its main theme being the conflict between his responsibility toward his wife and child, and his loyalty toward his native country. This theme runs throughout his prison diary.

The content of the diary closely reflects his often frustrating censored dialogue with his wife. Yoshiko and their only child Reika, were removed from Vancouver towards the end of October 1942 to join about five thousand Nikkei forming several camps in the Slocan Valley. Both in his diary and in letters to his wife, Miyazaki expressed his sense of guilt for neglecting his responsibility to his family. It seems that Yoshiko Miyazaki grew increasingly bitter with her situation in Slocan, especially after she finally realized that her dream to return to Japan, in a POW exchange ship, would never come to pass. Tension grew steadily between the couple interned in two camps separated by 2,000 kilometres. Eventually Yoshiko made up her mind, against her husband's wishes, to move to Eastern Canada with their daughter, where she found work as a house maid.

The *Mainichi Gurafu* article revealed some interesting aspects of Miyazaki's life. When he was a young man he was attracted to the writings of the romantic and nationalistic schools of literature and was fascinated by Inazo Nitobe's *Bushido* (The Way of the Samurai). According to the magazine article, when Miyazaki left Japan for North America he was filled with the secret desire of becoming a teacher like the famous Shoin Yoshida, one of the main idealogues of the anti-Shogunate nationalist rebellion leading to the Meiji restoration in 1868, the birth of the modern Japanese state. "I am a rightist," Miyazaki is reported to have asserted.

Miyazaki's manuscripts indicate that he devoted his last years to the study of Canadian history. He explains that the purpose of his solitary research was to better understand the problem of racial discrimination in North America, of which he himself was a victim, by tracing it back to its origins. He reached the conclusion that the persecution of native Indians by the white invaders was the fundamental problem of the entire history of Canada and therefore the key to understanding his own experience.

M E M O I R

That Morning

The cold, yellow, early December sun melted into the clean air through which the slowly travelling sound of the church bell announced Sunday morning mass. Having finished my late breakfast, I was absorbed in the sound of the bell. My daughter had gone to Sunday school and the living room was quiet without her. The sun on the piano keys was dazzlingly bright. Cigarette smoke turned mauve in the sun's rays and, swaying like seaweed in ocean currents, wafted up to the ceiling and disappeared. I noticed the subtle sound of the clock in the bookcase. It was 9:30. The church bell had stopped ringing and I imagined the people praying to God.

I turned on the 'Morning Serenade' radio program. I felt a suffocating shock and turned off the radio. I couldn't believe it. It was ridiculous. No, I will not believe it, I thought. My hands were trembling. I lit a cigarette and hurried to the kitchen where my wife was busy washing dishes.

"The war," I said. I think my voice was shaking. "Well?" she inquired. She didn't pay attention to me. "Japan . . . America," I said. Then she turned and asked, "What happened?"

I exclaimed impatiently, "Japan seems to have attacked Hawaii!"

Putting a plate on the counter, she said, "You must be joking."

I too wanted to believe that, so I said with some doubt, "Is it a mistake? But I think the radio said . . ." She could tell I wasn't sure. She said, "Yes, you heard it wrong because it was in English." She laughed and put her hands back into the soapy basin. She may be right, I thought. I wanted it to be so. Yes, it would be ridiculous in the middle of the Sino-Japanese war for such a thing to happen, I thought.

I went back into the living-room with my wife and turned on the radio. The angry voice leapt out at us: "Jap planes attacked Hawaii, Manila . . ." We just stood there without speaking. Every station was repeating the same thing. There was no doubt about it now. It was war!

"What's going to happen? Will Japan be alright? I'm asking you!" demanded my wife. "How am I supposed to know? I'm going to ask the office."[1] So I dialled the number and spoke to Mr. I. who didn't believe me. "What, America? This must be some kind of mistake. We haven't heard anything. What's gotten into you? Yes. I will be careful. Goodbye." The calm voice of Mr. I. ended there.

"That's what I thought," said my wife with a sigh of relief on the way back to the kitchen. "Nothing can happen so suddenly. It must have been a hoax." I heard the water running from the tap as if it was washing away all of our worries. However, the radio persistently repeated that Japanese planes had attacked. If this were a radio drama they would have used sound effects to recreate the sounds of a war, I thought. I found out that every radio station was repeating the same news. So as I became convinced that the beginning of the war was a reality, I was overwhelmed by the strange emotion that I was the only one in the world who possessed this very serious secret. I tried to control my adrenalin, but without success. My head was pounding. Impatiently I searched on the radio for conformation of the attack. The telephone rang loudly. My wife stood by me as if expecting the worst.

"It's true, it's true!" nervously blurted Mr. I. whose calm voice I had heard only moments before. "You are going to put out an extra edition, aren't you?" I asked him. "Well . . ." Mr. I. was at a loss for words.

I hung up. My wife remained silent. Soon the radio began to announce the sinking of the battleships *Arizona* and *Utah*. Then there was a special announcement telling all off-duty soldiers to get in touch with their regiments immediately. I felt the hustle and bustle of the war. I felt like myself again. Strangely, I felt very light and almost began whistling. Images of the mighty war planes, the bright red rising sun on their flanks as they flew over the Pacific, came to mind. This must be the turning point for the Japanese nation. This thought broke the peaceful silence of Sunday.

For a while I thought about nothing but Japan. I must have forgotten about Canada. It might have been an instinctive reaction nurtured by the many years of discrimination I had suffered here. When my daughter came back from church in her red coat, she handed a card to my wife. "Tadaima, Mama," she said. She was out of breath from running. On the card was a picture of Christ with holy verse printed below in colour. My wife unbuttoned her coat from behind, her arms around her.

"You ran, didn't you?" said my wife. "You must be careful. Did you behave well? Were you a good girl?" "Hai, Mama," she said, nodding. My wife blinked, her eyes brimming with tears, and embraced our daughter, squeezing her in her arms. Tears were glistening along her nose. As I watched my wife, my emotions almost exploded. Going to the window, I looked outside. It was so peaceful a morning you couldn't imagine a war.

That night I could not sleep. All the years I had spent in Canada came flooding back to me. They were all dry, dark and tasteless, like dead leaves. I realized that I had accumulated years without achieving any of the goals that I had set when I left Japan. The faces of my homeland came back to me. The silhouette of Hawaii on the horizon was still fresh in my mind. As a child I had always been told of the inevitability of war and now it was really happening. Fate, I thought. I also remembered those episodes where the Japanese people became angry with Americans prohibiting immigration from Japan and that there were those who swore to take revenge on Americans. The bloody drama between Japan and America which had become popularized among the common people was now to become a reality. Wasn't it an irony of destiny that I was going to experience it in this corner of the American continent?

Accept fate. Yes, that's right. Now that the Japanese nation was gambling with its fate, I too had to throw in my cards. Gambling is a matter of win or lose, I had to win. I would, without fear, bear the name of enemy alien and stand on the Canadian battle front. Yes, this was my fate. As an enemy alien I would be branded and deprived of my freedom. But nobody could take away the freedom and the desire to become a dignified enemy alien. This was my only strategy to fight my war, Although highly impractical, I would cling to it for dear life . . . I felt terrible that all my thoughts about the war overwhelmed my will power to the point that I couldn't sleep.

The next morning, after breakfast, my wife broke the silence. "Have you decided what you are going . . ." Tears welled up in my wife's eyes. "Well, I'm getting there." I replied. My wife did not say anything else, tears were running down her cheeks. My eyes misted over.

Spring Is Far

"This is S. calling." He held his breath and went quiet. All I could hear was the interference on the phone. I pushed the receiver against my ear and waited. "So, you are safe? Good," said S., finally. "I'm glad. Last night two Mounties suddenly appeared without warning at K.'s and told

Fairview Japanese Language School in Vancouver. Yoshiko Miyazaki is in the
top row (second from the left) with her husband Koichiro (fourth from the left).

Photo by Columbia Studio, courtesy of Reika Miyazaki

him to go with them. They said he would be able to return before long
and they did not give him any time to get ready . . . So I thought the
same thing might have happened to you. I'm happy it didn't.''

As I hung up I was impressed at how quickly the authorities had begun
to act. The image of K.'s amiable face came to mind. If the authorities
were intending on a lightning sweep then today might be my turn.
There was no time to waste. A shiver went down my spine, for a moment
I had an image of being arrested, lead away by a monstrous Mountie
while my wife and child were left to follow, dazed at what was
happening.

I began arranging my books and personal papers. I couldn't find
anything that might make the authorities suspicious of me. The only
things they might have been interested in were such books as Nippong-
Seishin-Ron and Kokki no Yurai by Shumei Okawa.[2] I had put personal papers
such as passports and licenses into a bag and gave it to my wife for safe
keeping.

"What are you going to do with those posters and pamphlets about
the China Incident?"[3] asked my wife, motioning me upstairs. I had
collected these during my visit to Japan. Certainly of anything that I
owned, they would draw the most suspicion. As I began to dispose of
the papers I was worried that any minute there would be a knock at the
door and I would be discovered. I would often stop, listen but there was
never anybody there.

I could no longer wait anxiously for the authorities to arrive, so I went
to my office. The atmosphere at the newspaper had changed radically.
Those who were busily running around in the office the previous day,
were all gathered in a small corner by the printers, talking in hushed
tones. Only the ringing of the telephone would shatter the quiet. I ran
up the stairs to the editorial office.

Everybody was idle, feet on their desks, leaning back in their chairs.
"No newspaper today," barked out the editor-in-chief, Mr. I. who was
cleaning his pipe. I felt as if I was greeting a friend whom I had not
seen for a very long time. A lot of time had passed in the day since Pearl
Harbour.

"Banned already? That was fast." I said with an indignant tone. "No.
It is not an order but because everyone is hyper-sensitive right now, we
decided to restrain from publishing. How about your language school?"
He added, as if intending to console me, "So what's happening with
the school?"[4] "We decided at last nights board meeting that we would

close down for the time being. But without the newspaper won't there be confusion in the community?" I was thinking about my fellow Issei, who were completely dependent on the Japanese-language newspapers. "I realize that," said the editor, "but the boss of the Japanese Standing Committee prefers that schools and newspapers of the community should restrain themselves." "Strange, nobody came to the school to tell me that. Did somebody come here to tell you?" I asked Mr. I. "I have just seen the 'King's' messenger[5] this morning," said Mr. I. contemptuously. That made me upset. "What right does he have to do that? It is such an interference. Is he a government officer or something?" "Well what can you do, when he says he represents the Mounties? . . . If we resist, you know the 'King' won't like it," said Mr. I. nonchalantly. "He won't like it? It's just an individual's opinion. It is not something that the Canadian government officially announced. It won't be too late to wait until we confirm with the authorities, will it?" I noticed that I was speaking as if I was the editor-in-chief. My compatriots would be lost in darkness without newspapers, like a ship without a captain. Groundless rumours and lies could push the people into a state of panic. Mr. I. finally said with bittersweet smile, "Let's have a couple of days rest and see what happens." I did not say anymore. Silence prevailed over the office.

It was the last day of the Japanese Language School. "The school will close today. Please continue to study Japanese little by little at home," I said. Three hundred pairs of eyes were looking at mine intensely. I tried to stop my voice from trembling. "The day when Japan and Canada are good friends will come again. You are all Canadians. Please become good Canadians. I can not tell you when I'll see you again, but it might be very soon. So let's wait for that day."[6] It became difficult for me to contain my tears so I quit speaking. After all the children had left, I looked around the empty classrooms — children's faces appeared at each desk. As I wondered when I would see them again I was overwhelmed by my pain. Although I had sounded optimistic in front of the children, I had no confidence in the words I had spoken. I went to the clean blackboard and scribbled, "Spring won't be too far away."

I went to the newspaper office every day. There was no sign of the paper reappearing. Day after day the office was cold and empty.

Slowly rumours of arrest were replaced by clearer information; according to Prime Minister King's announcement, the Mounted Police arrested forty-two Japanese as 'dangerous elements.' The reality of Pearl

Harbour also became much clearer. Our emotions were swinging back and forth like a pendulum. At the same time we were feeling closer and closer to the war. The English newspapers announced that more of the dangerous 'Jap elements' were being arrested.[6]

I worried about my colleagues being affected by my inevitable arrest, so I resigned from the school, cutting those ties. I sorted through my possessions in preparation for this eventuality. Since I was expecting to be arrested any day, I lived in continual anxiety. I threw the political posters and pamphlets I had obtained in Japan, as well as some other useless things I had, into the furnace. I spent half a day watching them turn to ash. I abused my nerves, expecting the worst, as if I was a Japanese spy. I was supposed to be preparing for a house search but the Mounties did not come quickly.

God Bless You

I felt I was in the shadows of normal society. It was March and spring was in full bloom. I felt the forced evacuation getting closer to me, as if I were being slowly suffocated. Japanese men of military age were being slowly rounded up and sent off to the snowy mountains. I was waiting for my turn. In my mind I knew I wouldn't be a pushover who would volunteer to go to a road camp for the sake of a pseudo-democracy. If the real reason for 'evacuating' the Japanese had been to protect them from violent mobs, they should have established special camps for the enemy aliens as was stipulated by international law. To me the idea of work camps were a smoke screen. I would prefer to live under the strict conditions imposed on prisoners of war. By living this way I would feel more connected to the war. Thus my mind was leaning toward refusing to go to work in a road camp.[7]

It was around this time my wife and I visited Mr. and Mrs. Wilkinson who had been teaching my wife conversational English. They served us tea and biscuits. "We came to say goodbye because we will soon depart for the snowy mountains," I said after sipping my tea. "Snow mountains? Where are they?" responded Mr. Wilkinson with his terse British accent while wiping his grey mustache with a napkin. "I mean Rockies," I said, "I hear the snow is three feet deep." The couple did not show any surprise as they were probably aware of the Japanese 'relocation'. "When are you leaving?" Mr. Wilkinson asked as if we were going for a vacation. "I have no idea, only the Mounties would know." "Well, even in the mountains there must be sufficient facilities. You shouldn't worry," said Mr. Wilkinson. "Well I hear there is no such thing. We are going to live in tents." "Oh that's too bad. But this is a war and everyone will experience hardships," said Mr. Wilkinson unemotionally. "There is nothing we can do, it must be God's will. You should obey the Canadian government. God go with you." According to Mr. and Mrs. Wilkinson everything was God's will. "I'm going to go anyway," I said, "but I refuse to believe that it is God's will. I go knowing that the war is an obscene, and cruel act perpetrated by human beings. The result of the war would decide . . ." I stopped there, feeling I was becoming too strong for the Wilkinsons. I changed my tone. "I don't know what will happen to my wife and child but they might need your help. Please watch over them." I stood up. Mr. and Mrs. Wilkinson took my hand and muttered, "God bless you." I was frustrated with their nonchalant attitudes. I knew we could not lose this war.

One night I asked my wife, "Will you be okay without me?" I thought she understood what I meant by these few words. "Yes. What else can I do? I'll manage." She was biting her lip. I tried to imagine what she and my child would have to go through. For a moment I felt that I didn't want to be the author of a tragedy. But as my wife put it, what else could I do?

My little daughter came down from upstairs in her pyjamas and said "Goodnight Mama, goodnight Papa," her dimpled smile beaming. As I watched them go upstairs, I imagined the day of separation was not far off. But I had no idea how many years would pass before I could see her again. Sitting with my head in my hands I remembered a recent scene at a family dinner. My daughter spotted tears in her mother's eyes; "Mama, are you crying?" Her eyes were wide with wonderment. "No, it's just smoke from the stove." It was painful to see my wife crying and smiling at the same time. "This stove is a bad girl, isn't it Mama?" We both forced a smile for the sake of our innocent child. I had to become strong.

No, Thank-you

Two Mounties arrived with a notice that said I had to report for a physical examination tomorrow. If I refused I would be interned. It was March 5.

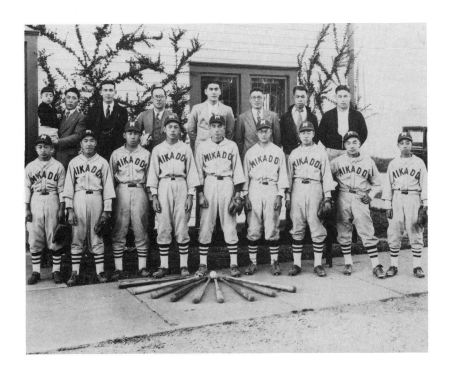

The Mikado, from the Fairview district of Vancouver, played in the same
junior class league as the Asahi, Fuso, and Yamato baseball teams.
(Koichiro Miyazaki is standing in back row, third from left.)

Courtesy of Reika Miyazaki

That night I stayed up late putting everything in order and packed, then I took a bath and finally went to bed. I was bothered by the thought that this would be my last night at home for a long time. I tossed and turned in bed as my thoughts ran wild.

Daylight appeared through a heavy mist of fine spring rain. My wife and young daughter came out to the sidewalk with me. The women next door came out too. The young leaves on the willow beside the gate were drooping in the rain, their undersides glistening silver. The black hair of my wife and child was full of moisture and droplets slid down their faces. I was pained to see my wife's face swollen with fatigue and grief. The neighbour said, with a smile, "Return safely," as if I was going out on an errand. Her innocent and simple manner annoyed me, but at the same time I felt bad for not letting her know that I wasn't coming back. I took my child's hand and shook it, saying goodbye several times. Then to my wife I began to say, "Well, I'm going. Please make sure . . . ," but I could not continue. She nodded, remaining silent and trying to hold back her tears. I began to walk along the wet sidewalk. As I turned the corner I looked back once to see my child's waving hand, white through the rain.

The hall at the Mounted Police headquarters was crowded with Japanese Canadian men. I saw many familiar faces. Dressed in formal clothes the men whispered together in little groups. Every once in a while uniformed police officers passed quickly through the crowds, their shiny riding boots clacking across the floor. The brightness of their red uniforms against the forest of dark clothes was strikingly beautiful.

"It's no use," several people complained. "After all, we all end up going." "Yeah, cowering with fear. No good we Japanese." "Those with big mouths all ended up quietly going to camps. Our race never cooperates."

These voices filled my ears. I remained silent and listened. Everybody is free to choose their own way. It is also their own will to go to a camp or not to. I felt like saying this to them but refrained. Each small group was expressing the same sorts of feelings. Lots of talking without real thinking or principles. They seemed to enjoy putting others down.

The physical examinations began. We were stripped naked. Men with rough and yellowish skin entered the brightly lit room and made an even uglier mass. In a way it was like a warehouse of cheap mannequins. Just as dolls are sold one by one, naked men lined up and disappeared one by one into the next room. The doctor wearing white, roughly examined our chest, genitals and anus and made us hurry with his calls of, "Next, next, next."

I knew that in the next room they were being made to sign a paper agreeing to work in the camps. I waited to be the last one to take off my clothes knowing that I wasn't going to sign. I didn't want to cause useless problems by holding up the line and making others wait. Above all, the last thing I wanted to do was influence others and have them mimic me. So I tried to remain inconspicuous until the end. Because nobody caused trouble things went smoothly and quickly as planned, and I was the last in line. This was the first time since I came to Canada that I was forced to undress. I was feeling an anger different from that which I had felt at the military physical examination in Japan. I stood in front of the doctor and he asked, peering over his eyeglasses, "Have you had any illnesses?" The question was so vague. I answered, "Sure." "How many times?" "Forgot." The doctor began to examine me as if he hadn't heard my answer. First the front and then back, making me bend over. As he said "okay" he turned on the tap and washed his hands with soap.

After I dressed I was called to a desk. A fat officer in street clothes stared at me from his chair behind the desk. Then, yawning, he counted the already-signed forms. His manner told me clearly that he was relieved to be almost done with the work. "Name, age, occupation, address," he asked mechanically and wrote the answers down. Then he said, "Sign here," pushing the paper towards me and staring up at me once more. I took the paper and pretended to read it. Then I said, "I can't. No, thank you," and I put the paper back on the desk. To this unexpected answer a look of surprise began to appear on his face. He then stood up and said authoritatively, "Why not? You have to." It was lunch time and he must have been hungry. I felt sorry to take his time for just me alone. "I will not." My voice sounded strangely high pitched.

Frowning, he pushed the buzzer. A uniformed officer and my friend T. appeared. Both T. and I were surprised to find each other in this strange place. "What's the matter?" T. asked me anxiously in Japanese. "I'm not going to the camp." The uniformed officer asked me why. I began to say, "I will not go to a place where there is no doctor . . . ," and he said, "In case of illness we'll call for a doctor. There's no need to worry." "And another reason, for democracy, I will not go. Road camps are not legal by international law. I have no experience of labour. I am sick." As I tried to express myself I thought my English sounded terrible. This was proven by the unconvinced faces of the officers. So I said in Japanese, "Anyway, I said no, I'm not going and I mean it!" I said this in a harsh tone as if T. was the person responsible.

T., who was not totally ignorant of my views, shook his head in discouragement towards the officers. He took on a neutral attitude, neither opposing or agreeing with me, and remained silent. The officer in street clothes looked at me and the other officer and said, "Can't help." He wrote something down, whispered into the other officer's ear and then left. I noticed that T. had also gone. I followed the uniformed officer into a small room in which there was a cell with iron bars. Without saying a word, he gestured at me to enter the cell.

The ceiling of the cell was so low my head almost touched it. Since there was no chair I remained standing. I touched the iron bars which were terribly cold and hard. I leaned against them and kept my eyes closed for a while. I smoked a cigarette but the guard didn't say anything. The white smoke drifted up slowly through the iron bars. The guard stole looks at me occasionally but remained silent. I began to feel hatred inside of me. I smoked cigarette after cigarette.

After a while the officer in street clothes came and took me to another room. There he told me once more to go to the camp, but I refused. He took my watch, pen, wallet, gloves, cigarettes, and matches and put them in a big paper bag before bringing me back to the cell.

For the first time I had become reduced to a man devoid of freedom and property. The first forty years of my life came to an end. I didn't feel that I was a victim of the war but rather of my own personality. This is, I thought, a man flirting with his own fate. In my black suit I must look like a bear pacing around the cell. How would my wife and child feel if they saw me? Those men who are departing for the camps tonight must be busy packing. And after all, what is it for, that I am locked up? As my thoughts wandered I felt dizzy. I was hungry and out of cigarettes. I felt a pain in my back and my legs felt numb. The guard looked bored. He peered through a window into the hall and talked with people passing by but he never spoke to me. I thought he might be waiting for me to speak to him but I remained as silent and closed as an oyster. His soft eyes purposefully avoided my hateful, burning eyes.

D I A R Y

March 7, 1942

I was put into a car, accompanied by two uniformed officers with guns and one plainclothes officer and we drove down Cambie Street. It was a peaceful and fine spring day. We came to Granville Street where the clock over Birks read one twenty-five. Soon we arrived at the immigration building. I was handed over to the soldiers who put me in a big room where there were ten compatriots, like myself, sitting around a table. A new life was in front of me. I wondered how long this could last.

I slowly explained to my friends what had happened to me since that morning. A discussion comparing one another's situations ensued. Soon I realized that I was terribly hungry. I was given some *sushi* which had been sent in to one of my friends. Instead of tea they poured cold water into an empty bottle. As I washed down the *sushi* with cold water, I was again acutely aware of this new stage in my life.

After nine o'clock I lay down in a bed. The bed was hard and there were no sheets. My head was filled with thoughts and I couldn't get to sleep. I remembered my family here and in Japan and I was ashamed that I was weeping. The reflection of the ocean on the ceiling, held images of my wife and daughter. To get away from the images I had to turn on my side resulting in my tears flowing over my cheeks.

So now I am a prisoner. I chose my path, making my family and myself suffer. I am after all an actor and author of my own tragedy.

March 8, 1942[9]

At seven o'clock in the morning some people began to get up, but I stayed in bed until nine o'clock staring into space. Breakfast was at eight and room cleaning was at nine thirty. This was my new routine. Some visitors began to arrive around ten o'clock and I asked one of them to give a message to my family. After two o'clock in the afternoon, Mr. O. brought my wife and daughter. The moment that I saw my daughter I felt my emotions welling up, so I stopped talking after saying hello. According to my wife, Reika burst into tears yesterday for no particular reason. The word orphan came to my mind. Forgive me, my wife, my daughter and I will give no excuses. I have accepted the invitation to hardship.

Since today is Sunday, there have been many visitors and they bring all kinds of different foods, and we eat as it is offered. At night as I lie down, I don't feel very good. We cannot continue this way. Tonight my main concern has been health but since I had received bed sheets and pyjamas, I fell asleep easily.

March 9, 1942

Our conversation is all about the Japanese community. We heard that since nine o'clock this morning cars owned by Japanese were confiscated by the government. The Japanese community is now without transportation. Cameras and the radios were prohibited today also. We are without sight or sound too. With my health in mind, today I refrained from snacking between meals.

March 10, 1942

My wife Yoshiko and my daughter visited. Was it just my imagination or was Reika depressed? She is only six years old but she might understand in her own way that her father is being taken away and that life will never the same. To my hello she responds very weakly. My wife prattled on about the events of the outside world. I hope that she can remain patient.

I received flowers and slippers. Mr. M. also visited me and he was talking about some kind of "responsibility." I wonder in such a crisis how many people could live up to the responsibility.

Supper was beef steak with rice. For the first time since arriving, I felt satisfied with a meal here.

March 11, 1942

It is drizzling. Leaning against the iron bars, I look down to the port below shrouded in fog. I feel a bit sentimental. I wonder how the outside world views me.

The rain stopped in the afternoon and the world is peaceful in the warm spring sunlight. Mr. A. visited me and gave me the Times, telling me to study hard. We had two new arrivals. Tonight everybody went to bed early.

March 12, 1942

Rain. In the afternoon Yoshiko and Reika visited me. They brought bean rice and a *shakuhachi* flute. My wife seemed to be very worried about my reputation and what people were saying about me. I spent hours looking down as dozens of military vehicles passed by.

March 13, 1942

Rained all day. It's extremely gloomy. In the morning T. came to visit me, informing me of what is happening in the community. I admire his passion. I received *Life* magazine and cigarettes.

March 14, 1942

Good weather. Just after lunch my wife and Reika came by. I was relieved to see that Reika was more cheerful than her last visit. They brought me *miso* soup in a thermos but I didn't want to enjoy it alone so I asked them to take it back. I also received sheets and shirts.

Mr. M. visited and I asked what the situation was in the Japanese community. Let those who want to handle the situation handle it and we'll see what happens.

March 15, 1942

We were sleeping in as usual when we were awakened and told that we were moving. I took breakfast which I usually don't have and began to pack my things. While we were packing an officer came in and shouted at us to "Hurry up boys!" I was awake and finally it was clear that we were being shipped out. Before leaving we were taken out of the room and searched and they even went through our hair.

We boarded the train. Each door was guarded by two armed military police. There was no time even to inform my family. Five minutes past ten in the morning, the train carrying prisoners pulled out of the station heading for the East. Goodbye Vancouver, my family and my friends.

The train roared along beside the Fraser River, zigzagging through the Fraser Valley. Just before eleven o'clock the porter distributed what appeared to be food for the day: one loaf of bread, one can of sardines, one can of salmon, two apples and some baloney. The quantity of food gave us some idea of the distance we would be travelling. We were thirteen in one coach so there was a lot of room. The train laboured up the steep gorges. I got tired of watching the world pass by the window, so I closed my eyes and tried to focus my attention on the war and my personal situation. I find that I can't concentrate on anything except for the fact that I'm going East. My family must be anxious not knowing what has or will happen to me. I felt responsible for that.

At daybreak, I wake up and I'm still on the moving train. We are in the middle of the Rocky Mountains, that I had once before travelled. Seven a.m. we crossed the border between B.C. and Alberta. The snow-covered Rockies, half in purple shadow and half in sun are silent despite their grandeur. I see many deer on the mountain sides. Soon after passing Banff, I asked one of the officers to send a telegram to my family. Ten o'clock we finally arrive at a deserted, desolate station where we were transferred onto military trucks which then took us to the camp. The first thing I noticed was the painted red circles on the backs of each prison uniform.[10] Among the many prisoners I could distinguish a group of Japanese.

After searching our belongings and being addressed by the director of the camp, we were finally taken to our barracks. Exhausted.[11]

March 16, 1942

Clear. Reveille was at six-thirty. We could not sleep in as we did at the Immigration Building in Vancouver. I was so sleepy. Seven thirty breakfast, eight o'clock roll call and there was another search through our belongings. In the afternoon we were given our camp uniforms . . . The shirt has a large red circle on the back and the pants have thick red stripes down each leg. I still feel tired. I hear this camp is almost governed by the German prisoners. Lunch was at twelve o'clock, dinner was at five o'clock and there is a curfew at nine o'clock and at ten o'clock all the lights have to be turned off.

March 18, 1942

Clear. In the morning, my wallet and razor were returned, two of the things that had been taken away by the Mounties. I enjoyed shaving after such a long time. In the afternoon there was a physical examination. The doctor said something was wrong with my throat and gave me medicine. At night I played the *shakuhachi* flute which I hadn't played for a long time. Later I went to watch the Germans doing their calisthenics. I was impressed by their discipline.

March 19, 1942

Clear. There was a morning inspection by the director of the camp. I played *shakuhachi* flute. In the afternoon we were allowed to play records so we asked the Germans to fix our broken-down record player. After a long absence I heard the sound of recorded music once again. After supper I visited a friend in another barracks.

March 20, 1942

Clear. Last night, thoughts about my family invaded my sleep for about two hours. In the morning I watched the Germans doing their exercises and in the afternoon I visited the other barracks. After supper I went to the concert given by the Germans. I was moved and overwhelmed at how good the band and music were. I learned two German words, (thank you and goodbye). As I lie here in bed the strong wind is blowing against our barracks.

March 22, 1942

It snowed all day. The temperature is high and therefore the snow is soft and wet. Already a week has passed since I was moved from the immigration building to here. Although a whole week has gone by I am numb to the passing of time. Since today is Sunday, the time schedule has slacked off slightly which makes for a confusing day. In the afternoon I continued to read a book called *North America*.

March 23, 1942

At eleven o'clock I went with M. and O. to talk with the director of the camp concerning the labour of our fellow prisoners. He insisted that rules would dominate. On our return to the barracks we reported on the meeting to our fellow prisoners. We decided to begin working from tomorrow on. We were given rubber boots and gloves for our jobs. At night I contemplated work. After all we are prisoners deprived of freedom. We are all dependent on laws negotiated between nations.

March 24, 1942

Eight-thirty. I dressed in the unfamiliar clothes and went off to work. Following another body search by the guards I walked over to the soldiers' barracks. Our assigned work involved digging out and removing large tree stumps. Although it was minus twelve I didn't feel cold. In the afternoon we carried firewood. Around three o'clock there was a heavy snow fall. Prisoners branded by the big red circle silently pushed their wheelbarrows through the heavy snowfall. This was an image of war . . . If my wife and my daughter could see me in this crowd, being forced to work, what would they feel?

I feel good after the hard day's work. After supper I lied down for a while. I was grateful just to be eating an apple during these hard times when vegetables and fruits are in such short supply. I had never appreciated an apple so much. It was like a treasure I had never noticed.

March 25, 1942

The mundane life of the camp is offset by the gorgeous Rocky Mountains which loom above us, framed by a deep blue sky. Minus two degrees. I visited camp 5A and 8B and they offered me rice crackers and candy. Six thirty p.m. I went to see a motion picture for five cents. But my thoughts were not on the motion picture. How long could I continue this life . . .

March 29, 1942

Sunday. In the morning I read some old magazines and took my laundry to be done. In the afternoon I saw another motion picture called The Hunchback of Notre Dame. Maybe because of the electricity shortage the motion picture was too dark but this softened the harsh reality of the story. After roll call our Japanese group held a meeting which became so heated that it was thrown into turmoil. All that just to elect a new representative; Mr. Tanaka took the position temporarily.

Mailed a letter to my family.

March 30, 1942

Temperature rose. Most of the snow on the ground melted leaving a terrible mess of mud and water. The military newsletter was distributed . . .

During my nap I had a dream about my wife which caused me to wake with a start. I prayed that nothing bad is happening to her. I was in a daze. I went out, took some remaining snow and put it into my mouth. The coldness made me remember even more.

April 4, 1942

The snow which began around ten o'clock last night had stopped by the time I got up. Again the world was blanketed with white but by the mid-afternoon it had again melted leaving a mess of mud. I washed a handkerchief, a pair of socks and a piece of clothing. Before supper I was walking in front of the office when I was given a long-awaited letter from my family. I had trouble opening the letter because my hands were shaking. As I began to read my eyes misted over, I was shocked to read that Reika's birthday was soon. Because it took so long for the letter to reach me, her birthday had already gone by. The fact that I didn't even remember her birthday, made me feel guilty. But simply receiving the letter was a relief. Night in the high country, stars shine bright. From the silhouette of the camp barracks dozens of white string-like wisps of smoke rise to the heavens.

April 5, 1942

Easter Sunday. For breakfast we had two Easter eggs and cake. Both lunch and supper were an exceptional treat. On top of that, presents arrived: cigarettes, handkerchiefs, biscuits, and soap. The cigarettes I had brought from Vancouver were just about finished, so I was happy. I hear these presents are from the German officers group, a German prisoner aid group in the U.S., the American and Canadian Red Cross, and Captain S. One thirty in the afternoon there was a free movie but it was awful. Six thirty I went to see the Germans who were putting on an acrobatic exhibition. I really admire their discipline and order. It was very professional, using music and simple lighting. Snow began to fall around three and is still falling as I write.

April 8, 1942

Another day of labour. After yesterday's hard work I went outside with reluctance. I found out that today's work is to pull nails from the old lumber we piled yesterday. Twenty people pour their energy into this one thing.

After the morning's work we were told on our return that in two days Japanese prisoners would be moved so we had to get ready. I went into our barracks and each person had a different idea of where we would be going. The atmosphere was cheerful and optimistic. After lunch there was another physical examination but they only checked our backs. The work in the afternoon was the same thing but the time somehow passed quickly. Our impending move made us feel like school kids before a field trip. Everyone was cheerful today and even our guard was nicer. It was a pleasant afternoon.

We had loaned our record player to the Germans and as a show of gratitude they made us handmade picture frames. As a souvenir I asked the Germans to carve the camp name, their names and addresses on them.

April 10, 1942

Clear and sunny. This is the day to bid farewell to the Kananaskis camp. We were told to be ready by two o'clock. In the morning we were all busy packing. By three o'clock we put all the bags in front of the main gate. We were all ready to go. I noticed that I hadn't done my usual walk of the camp, so took a shorter one. I stood on higher ground on the south side and looked over the camp and remembered the days that I had spent here. Small clouds were moving in the sky like a herd of sheep . . .

Four-thirty. The Japanese had an early supper and we shook hands with the German workers from the dining hall and went out to the gate. The Germans gathered in a group to say farewell. Finally the trucks arrived. Each truck held ten people. There were some who called out *Banzai*, before getting into the truck. As the trucks pulled out we were covered by a huge cloud of dust.

After waiting half an hour for the train it finally arrived. Even while on the train we were heavily guarded. The camp director was there either to see us off or to direct the guards. Seven fifteen the train pulled out of the station and continued on through the copper-coloured terrain carrying the fate of fifty-three people. Around eight o'clock we were in Calgary. We had a long wait there.

April 11, 1942

I woke up at seven thirty and we were at Moose Jaw. At nine o'clock we were arriving in Regina and then the train continued on through barren, monotonous countryside.

April 12, 1942

I woke up and we were in Port Arthur, Ontario. The station is by the lake which is so large it looks like the ocean. I think I had heard the name of this station while still back in Japan. The ice on the lake sparkles brightly in the morning sun. From there the train ran along the lakeshore. We had lunch at Jackfish, near Schreiber station. I spotted Japanese road camp workers at the edge of the railway tracks. Five or six young guys with towels around their necks vaguely watched the train go by. Inside the train we shouted that we were Japanese and banged the window but it wasn't clear whether those guys noticed us.

April 13, 1942

Four o'clock in the morning at Sudbury we began travelling again. Six o'clock we were at Chalk River. At seven thirty we got off at Petawawa. As usual there are many soldiers waiting for us. We got into the truck which ran forty or fifty minutes through as birch tree forest. As we neared our destination, I heard the clamour of a loud welcome. We guessed that there must be some Japanese already at the camp. But behind the barbed wire, we found the place was crowded with Germans and Italians who were chanting: *Tojo Banzai, Yamashita Banzai, Japan Banzai.* This unexpected welcome made us feel like returning heros.

We waited in a large empty room which had walls covered with pin-up girls. From these pictures I could guess the general atmosphere of the camp. We were thoroughly searched. The military doctor upset me by examining my genitals with a cane. Then there were admission forms to fill out. Finally we were taken into barrack number eight, where I was to begin my new life.

It was too late to have lunch and we were told we'd have to get something for ourselves. Some volunteers prepared coffee and bread for us. For supper we also had to fend for ourselves. Here we seem to be expected to govern our own affairs. After supper I took a shower and washed off the sweat and dirt of three days and three nights on the train. I was so refreshed. I was almost reborn.

April 14, 1942

Clear and sunny. We spent all day cleaning the barracks. After supper we were surprised when a huge, boisterous chorus approached us from the other side of the fence. It turned out to be a warm welcome from the Germans and Italians carrying Japanese navy flags and playing accordions and other instruments. When the singing swelled to thunderous crescendo, the Sergeant-Major ordered us to go back into the barracks. Without saluting we simply obeyed his order. For a while after this incident our barracks were locked and I suppose the Germans and Italians gave up and had to go to their barracks. I wrote to my family.

April 15, 1942

Rain. I haven't seen rain for a long time. As I look into the birch forest it is shrouded with a gentle spring rain. It is all very dream-like. My diaries, which were confiscated, were returned cut up and censored.[12] It is just an internee's diary. Do they have the right to do such things? At least they should give some reasons. They can confiscate my diaries but the facts of my life will not disappear.

The supper was sukiyaki with rice. Everyone's delight at the meal was beyond description. Some even ate two big bowls of rice, although I couldn't even finish one, I felt so happy just to see and taste rice; it was delicious. The rice was sent from Mr. M.'s house.

April 17, 1942

I washed four pieces of clothing which was such work that I perspired a lot. Since it rained in the afternoon I had to put my laundry inside and then outside. My wife's letter arrived, dated April 9. Reika is well, my wife is well and busy. I was relieved at the news. My letters seem to have been reaching her. After supper I discussed with the others about the problem of labour. My opinion was not taken seriously. Their negative attitudes really bothered me. I am afraid that people who can think seriously are getting scarce.

April 19, 1942

Peaceful Sunday. Around ten o'clock in the morning, I received two letters from my Yoshiko. Reika's letter, with childish handwriting, was included. As I read I was so excited that I didn't notice the tears in my eyes. Reika's writing was all in katakana alphabet which she had probably learned from her mother, these were the first signs that could express her heart and mind. What a precious gift to her father. Yoshiko described Reika's birthday party that Miss Snowdon, her piano teacher, kindly organized. I felt so grateful for the warm hearts of the Snowdon family who love Reika so much. The English family who could do so much for the mother and child of enemy aliens. This must be the true English spirit. I felt light-hearted all day and kept on reading the letter over again and imagining my family and each person of the Snowdon family. My wife also sent me thirty dollars.

Koichiro Miyazaki and daughter Reika welcoming King George and
Queen Elizabeth on their royal visit to Vancouver, May 29, 1939.

Courtesy of Reika Miyazaki

April 20, 1942

Today was the first day of work (digging holes for the garbage), but my turn didn't come. I spent the day idle in the barracks. I flipped through a Japanese book but it didn't really capture my interest. So in the afternoon I borrowed the *Montreal Gazette* and the *Toronto Daily Star* from the office and read them from cover to cover. The big news was the English bombing of France.

I made a notebook cover out of birch bark; I wanted to write a nice phrase but nothing came to me. Even after going to bed I kept thinking, but nothing. Just as I was falling asleep I came up with the idea of attaching Reika's letter to the cover.

April 26, 1942

There was an announcement that the day after tomorrow about one hundred more Japanese will arrive at the camp. There must be many that I know, I can hardly wait. In the afternoon there was a committee meeting. I am a member but I did not go. A. came back and reported to me but some things were unclear and as a result we asked our leader, Tanaka, to come to our barracks after supper to explain.

My wife's letter inquires as to disposing of our furniture back home. I wrote her back.

April 28, 1942

Cloudy. After seven-thirty in the morning we were forbidden to leave our barracks. Just after eight o'clock, trucks loaded with new prisoners began to arrive. All lined up at the window looking out, when anyone spots somebody they know we call out their names or cry out with joy. Around noon after going through their physical the new arrivals were lined up outside and we lined up a short distance away from them. Almost at once everybody started talking very loudly. The guards told us to quiet down and we did but the silence never lasted more than a few minutes. The talking started up again. I was relieved to find E. and T. T.'s father was not there but I found out that he had been sent from the Immigration Building to the municipal hospital. Since I had been very worried about his father's health, now I feel better to know that he stayed in the hospital instead of travelling all this way. All afternoon we were all very busy exchanging information. By the end of the day I was exhausted.

April 29, 1942

Cloudy. From eight-thirty in the morning we held a worship ceremony of *Tencho-setsu* [the Emperor's birthday]. We all saluted while watching the sun dance into a new day over the birch forest and we sang *Kimigayo* [Japan's national anthem]. It was a solemn moment and I felt very refreshed. This was to be one of the most memorable *Tencho-setsu* for me to have the honour of celebrating.

April 30, 1942

We held an unscheduled committee meeting to discuss the kitchen trouble. Since our legitimate demands for reform had been rejected by the authorities and the kitchen workers had resigned, the committee had decided to support their resignation and start a hunger strike beginning the next morning. It would continue until they accept our demands. Inside I felt these actions to be slightly excessive but I went along with the committee.

May 1, 1942

The hunger strike started. Even the young energetic ones refrained from exercise to be ready for the strike. Around ten o'clock a response came from the assistant director. We held a general meeting and decided that the response was not satisfactory and we would continue with the strike. One o'clock and I took a nap. Around four o'clock we held another general meeting. A Colonel from the military camp came and accepted our demands. We unanimously accepted the Colonel's response and voted to stop the hunger strike. Everybody looked very happy and the meeting turned into an almost festive occasion. Around seven o'clock we had supper. This was a happy ending for the first hunger strike that I have ever experienced. After supper I went to enjoy the record concerts given by the Italians.

May 4, 1942

In the morning it was cloudy but as we trudged out with shovels over our shoulders, the weather cleared up and there was a nice spring breeze. For me this was the first day of work at Petawawa. We were given the job of clearing land. We were supposed to work in the afternoon as well but as the Spanish consul came to visit. I went to the meeting as a representative. We raised ten questions which included family relief, resettlement and labour. But we didn't get any specific answers. It was a bit disappointing but this was just our first meeting and since this was the first meeting and very formal I still have hope that later meetings will go better.

May 5, 1942

Today is *sekku* [Boys' Day]. There are no banners or fish decorations to put up, but my spirits were lifted.[13] A small package from my wife arrived. There was a can of salty beans so I immediately shared it with everybody. Even this is a very special treat for me. Before supper I read *Oku no Hosomichi*.[14] I made up seven or eight *haiku* poems, although I don't know if they are qualified to be. I feel my present circumstances somehow made me closer to the wandering poet, Basho. After supper I sumo-wrestled with some of the young men; for the first time in ten years. By the end I was exhausted and really felt my age.

May 10, 1942

Morning and night it gets cold as if we are thrown back to winter. But during the day the sun beats down so strongly that one can get dizzy. I put on sunglasses and read *Horoki* [Hobo's Journal]. With a slight breeze many white-cotton-like maple seeds flew through the air and fell on the page of my book. After supper I walked around the track many times and I suddenly remembered the sky of my native country. The clouds were immobile over the birch woods; this cloud, that cloud, each one somehow brought me back to my country.

The newspaper reports that the battle of the Coral Sea ended in defeat for the Japanese navy. The room was abuzz from the rumours about the Japanese defeat. But the *Toronto Daily Star* had articles by military critics who analyzed the complexities of the battle. I guess ordinary *keto* would only be excited by the news and not realize the complex nature of war battles.[15]

May 19, 1942

Seven large tents were set-up which we think means that more Japanese will be arriving tomorrow.

May 20, 1942

After breakfast as I went out and saw a convoy of automobiles on the other side of the lake. As we began to get excited and cried out: "the Japanese are coming" etc., the soldiers ordered us back to the barracks.

We decided to be less noisy than last time as we peeked out the windows.

May 21, 1942
From the new arrivals I heard about the situation in Vancouver. Since I left there the influence of the gang has been great.[16] As I heard the news I could not help but laugh.

It was a very cold night.

May 22, 1942
Rain. It has been raining hard all day. The rain dampens my imagination and I only feel terrible when I imagine those guys in the tents.

May 23, 1942
A gloomy day. In the morning I read and in the afternoon I was awakened from my nap to receive a telegram from Vancouver. It was from a person I didn't know telling me that Nishio was appointed a liaison committee member instead of Charlie Tanaka. This committee, led by Morii, is cooperating with the government.[17] It was unexpected news. After discussing with camp leaders I sent the following telegram: "Thanks for your telegram. Our meeting decided that we oppose the appointment of Nishio. We also will inform Mr. Nishio of this. We recommend Charlie Tanaka. Good luck."

At meal time I explained about this to everybody.

May 25, 1942
When I was hanging around in the workshop I heard a rumour that somebody by the name of T. died. As I hurriedly walked to see H.T., he was crossing the yard on his way to see me. He showed me a telegram. I began to cry as I read about his father's death. I could not find words to console him.[16]

I participated in the executive board meeting after supper. From seven o'clock we held a memorial meeting in the dining hall. We all swore over T.'s dead body that we would continue to go forward, learning a lesson from his death.

May 30, 1942
All day I remained idle. The camp committee meeting after lunch discussed, among other things, the problem of resignations and how to handle them.

May 31, 1942

I went with our camp leader, Tanaka, to talk to the two members who wish to resign and we tried to persuade them to stay.

After supper [the same group of people] came to visit me and now, in turn, they wanted to persuade me to become their advisor. I agreed that I was in a position to serve them but I nonetheless declined to accept such a difficult job. But they insisted that in this crisis they needed my help just as a friend. So finally I could do nothing but accept their offer. I really wonder if I could become a good advisor for their group. I must study hard.

June 1, 1942

Today a Japanese language school began in our camp.

June 2, 1942

Cloudy. I taught Japanese to Nisei at a grade six level. All my students are without exception very serious.

I was asked to read the pamphlet of the Nisei Mass Evacuation Group.[19] The logic was very clear but I felt that something was lacking.

June 13, 1942

Among those 295 who are detained, today for the first time one person was released. I hear that he had been applying for release. If this leads to happiness, I'd only like to congratulate him and wish him luck on his future.

June 19, 1942

I pulled radishes and washed them. They were much bigger and much redder than the ones that I pulled the other day.

I was asked for advice concerning the letter of appeal the Nisei Mass Evacuation Group is going to send to Ottawa. I emphasized to them that they should add a protest against the unjust treatment of the Nisei including those who happened to be born in Japan when their parents were visiting.

In the afternoon I had a headache, maybe I caught a cold. Everybody went to see a motion picture but I stayed in bed and read the newspaper. An article reports that Japanese in a road camp in the Kamloops area organized a demonstration against the foreman of the camp.

I received a letter from my wife complaining that my letters don't arrive often enough. She demands at least one letter every week. That's what I have been doing. T. came with *yokan* [bean cake] that he had received from my wife. I was grateful for Yoshiko's thoughtfulness.

June 23, 1942

When I came back from school, two letters from my wife were waiting for me. One letter was full of her frustration and anger, saying that since I don't write she is going to stop writing to me. The other one is explaining her attitude in detail toward Mr. Nishio. After reading them I felt so depressed for the rest of the day. I have been writing at least once a week, but I guess they haven't arrived. As to her attitude toward Mr. Nishio, it's for her to decide, so I don't say anything. Later I received a telegram from her telling me to trust her. I could see very well that she too is suffering. On top of that one pair of pyjamas, two cans of tea and text books arrived. It reminded me of her love and care for me.

July 1, 1942

It was like a dream. Last night, sometime after one o'clock, the sound of gunshots rang out and those sounds still echo in my ears. In the morning the information about what happened that night slowly unfolded. It was something that I didn't expect at all.[20]

After breakfast everyone gathered in front of barracks no. 7 and no. 8 and the hut leaders held a discussion and we decided to protest against the previous evening's unjust shootings by the guards. The refusal to participate in roll call spread slowly over the camp like a tide. An appeal for an interview was sent to the director of the camp. Later we had a general meeting to discuss the matter. Seven people were selected as representatives and sent to the director's office to negotiate. But the authorities insisted that the responsibility lay with the Japanese. There was nothing to negotiate. After lunch we had another meeting and to protest the shootings decided to refuse roll calls until the time the Spanish consul visits the camp again. There was no roll call in the evening. In retaliation the authorities refused to bring in the newspapers.

July 4, 1942

The Petawawa camp director came in the afternoon to deal with the situation. The director thought it was too late for any negotiations and decided on harsh action. Many officers, including himself, came to the compound, met the hut leaders and read the military laws and rules for prisoners of war. Without giving us a chance to ask questions or give opinions they ordered us to comply with roll calls within five minutes. If we did not comply, they declared, we would be shot or given punishment up to a life sentence. Our spokesman reported to us what the authorities had said and consulted with the 300 Japanese prisoners. We decided that we had no choice but to accept. But as our answer was given to the director he immediately pulled out a list of names. He named ten people who were ordered to be arrested. They were taken away. They disappeared as we chanted *ganbare*, encouraging them to be strong.[21]

The routine of roll call was reestablished but we were still left with the issue of protest against the illegal shooting. I realized from today's incident that people are not very strong when threatened with immediate action. I wonder what my face looked like then. But the faces I saw around me could not hide their fear. Maybe we were all too excited.

After role call the hut leaders met and elected a negotiating team and hoped to work toward release of the ten men arrested. Before the evening roll call I reported to my barracks about the meeting and asked for ten cents from the men.

July 5, 1942

Overcast Sunday. Probably because of yesterday's trouble our yard is very quiet. We sent out the belongings of the ten arrested. I helped pack O.'s belongings and then I pondered the word "sacrifice."

In the afternoon I was asked to be present in a Nisei discussion meeting. We talked about the issue of Mass Evacuation. It was a peaceful meeting.

July 16, 1942

I am carving something out of wood. Each time I make a carving mistake I feel very disappointed. Lazy day. The result of the battle of Midway was announced. On the American side the aircraft carrier *Yorktown* and a destroyer went down; on the Japanese side sixteen ships, including four aircraft carriers and dozens of airplanes were lost. If this is true, it is a complete defeat for the Japanese. There was a motion picture tonight after supper but I did not go.

July 17, 1942 (Petawawa)

We were preparing for the *obon* celebration.[21] There was a rumour that we might be transferred soon. Some people said, "No, it's just for Italians and Germans." At lunchtime Tanaka, the camp spokesman, announced that we were going to the Angler camp on Monday at 8:00 a.m. to join other Japanese. Thus the rumour turned out to be true. Here and there people began to suddenly talk about moving. It has been four months here. Now that I know I'm moving soon I feel very nostalgic uttering the word Petawawa. I told my wife without delay about the transfer. It seems that everybody has begun to feel excited as if we were going on a school trip. Music began to come from the record player. Nervous excitement filled the room. We will be closer to Vancouver and to Japan. This vain hope came to us. After supper I played *Go* and read the *Gazette*.

July 18, 1942

As some people rushed to pack right after breakfast the barracks became noisy and messy and then everybody joined in. We were supposed to bring our luggage out at 1:30 but nothing happened until evening so we had to bring our things back inside. The heat became unbearable. I think it is a record heat this year. It seems that there was a death among the Germans. When the hearse arrived I went to watch their exercise area. The men were all lined up. As the hearse began to move they made the German-style salute. Not a soul accompanied the hearse. I felt a deep sorrow. Letter from my wife. There were tinted photographs of my daughter inside. My wife says, "On your birthday we missed you, though you must have forgotten it." I forgot it indeed! After evening roll call it was so hot that many stayed outside.

July 19, 1942

This is the last day of our life at Petawawa internment camp. I remember the day we arrived here when the camp was still surrounded by the harsh, bleak winter. The lake was frozen white. The biting wind was blowing. The ground was hard and icy. The birch forest gave a bleak impression of white skeletons and made us shiver. The whiteness of the landscape is still clearly imprinted in the back of my mind. It so happens that we are leaving here in the middle of summer. Tomorrow morning we are leaving this place for good. The camp is now surrounded by lush green . . . Many people have cleared the barren land and sowed various vegetables and flowers which our eyes and stomachs have begun to enjoy. Well, I'd better stop being sentimental. Tomorrow a new struggle begins in a new camp . . .

O., N., and K. who had been detained for three days came back. They say they were treated brutally. Anyhow, their return makes our minds peaceful.

Supper was something resembling chop suey accompanied by rice. After seven the heat was interrupted by an evening thunderstorm. I hope that the terrible heat may be cooled down. We are going to get up at 4:30 tomorrow morning.

July 20, 1942

Woke up at 4:30. It was still dark. Had a simple breakfast and then roll call at 5:30. We were supposed to depart at 6:30 but it didn't seem possible. I lay down on the bed and contemplated moments of Petawawa. Trucks began to arrive. First the Germans and Italians boarded the trucks. As they were leaving we shouted and waved goodbye. The seriousness of the soldiers and the exaggerated number of them made me laugh. Twenty-eight of us in one truck departed around eight. Goodbye, Petawawa Camp. Goodbye, flowers, grass, and birds.

We had to wait for one hour near the train depot where we had gotten off on our arrival. I was overcome with sleepiness. Some of the soldiers began to sing and got out to pick wild berries. The seriousness of their guarding became dubious.

The train departed at 11:00. At Chalk River, curious children came up close to see us. They glared at me belligerently through the train window, perhaps drawn by my mustache. I thought it was comic.

July 21, 1942

Around four-thirty I woke up and soon after we had breakfast. Around six o'clock the train stopped. Through the windows we can see a camp. This is Angler, where we are going to live.

The camp was built on a sandy hill. We rested in the dining hall. Those Japanese who had arrived before us were looking at us from outside. The guards gave our luggage a thorough search but I had nothing of any interest to them. Looking at the frame that I had made from birch bark, one chaplain said to me in Japanese, "You are very skilled with your hands." I was surprised to hear this man speaking Japanese. The physical was also very thorough and strict. Those with athletes foot were left behind. I was given a sheet of paper with a bed number on it. I went into my barracks which is no. 4A. My former students from Vancouver who had arrived earlier came to visit me. We hadn't seen each other for a long time It was a very pleasant visit. They all told me how heavily this camp is guarded. They wanted to know my impression of the Petawawa camp . . .

At ten-thirty they turned the light off and I immediately fell asleep. I was awakened around midnight by a soldier who came to do roll call.

July 23, 1942

It is becoming clear that the life at this camp will be much tougher. I really wonder if all this is necessary for civilians like us. I'm already missing the relaxed atmosphere of the Petawawa life.

July 27, 1942

There was a heavy fog this morning. The way people stood for morning roll call resembled an ink drawing. I talked to Mr. H. and other educators about fund-raising for education. The sky cleared in the afternoon. My former students from Vancouver got together and discussed the future of the Nisei Mass Evacuation Group.

Letter from my wife. It tells me that Reika passed the music exam with honours. A newspaper article about that was enclosed. I could imagine Yoshiko's joy, impossible to be fully contained within the letter. She seems to have been moved by my concern about their relocation to the interior camp. Her emotional writing moves me but as I read this type of letter I tend to feel depressed. I guess I just wish that I could share the joy with them. I cannot bear the sharp contrast between joy and sorrow.

The Petawawa group was summoned to the camp leader's office to explain the details and sequence of events of the Petawawa incident to the camp leaders. I was summoned too.

July 30, 1942

It was kind of chilly all day. I wrote to my wife telling her that this camp is worse than Petawawa. I also sent a postcard to Reika congratulating her for her success with the piano exam. This was the first letter independent of my wife's which I sent to my daughter.

There was an incident where a guard kicked an internee while he was working. We decided to file a grievance and meet the administrator and sub-director of the camp . . .

Evening roll call was done inside because of the rain.

*A snapshot of a Sho-kokumin or Little Patriot sent from Japan
before the war to Koichiro Miyazaki by one of his relatives.*

Courtesy of Reika Miyazaki.

July 31, 1942

I was told that after roll call the authorities made an announcement regarding yesterdays incident. One internee stepped up and began to protest but was immediately taken away by the guards. But still the whole picture is not very clear . . .

August 3, 1942

I read an old issue of Fuji magazine. I was writing a letter to my wife when I received a registered letter from her. She is worried about me ever since she received my first letter from Angler. Reika is sensitive and sometimes without reason she says; "Daddy" and then begins crying. My wife wants to know more details about the Petawawa incident. A short part of the letter was written by Reika herself. Her hand writing has improved and is now quite strong. She says; "Daddy, when you come home let us all go back to Japan." I imagine the kind of conversations she must be having with my wife. This was moving to me. I tried to picture their quiet life without me. I wrote them back saying that life here seems empty but it is worthwhile because I believe that step by step I am climbing the hill to make myself truly Japanese.

August 4, 1942

Clear. After lunch I was idle until I heard that the Spanish consul would visit later in the day. So immediately eighty-one Issei gathered and discussed what we would ask and tell the consul. Ten people, including myself, were elected as representatives for the discussion with the consul.

After supper we had a meeting with the consul in the recreation room. After each man shook hands with him, we presented twenty questions. Unlike in Petawawa the military was not present, so the meeting was very free and relaxed. But the information concerning POW exchanges which we were most anxious to know about was uncertain and we were all very disappointed in that.

August 12, 1942

After lunch a small rumour concerning the way the authorities were handling the mail, developed into an incident where internees surrounded the post office. Hut meetings were held to discuss what had happened. It was concluded that in order to avoid unnecessary suspicion, the Japanese will not involve themselves in processing outgoing mail, leaving everything to the authorities.

Wrote a letter to my wife. I asked her to explain in a way that I would understand what kind of 'drastic measures' she is threatening to take in terms of her relocation.

August 18, 1942

In the morning I received a letter from my wife. Reika received a five dollar cheque from a *hakujin* woman to encourage her piano skills. People say that there are no borders in the world of art. I was moved by this woman's warm heart toward the daughter of enemy aliens.

August 21, 1942

In the afternoon we heard the news that the warring nations reached an agreement on the POW exchanges. Soon the Director's notice reached us telling those who wish to go to Japan to apply, thus confirming the news reports. Everybody spent the whole afternoon discussing the possibilities. But I wonder what the Nisei are feeling?

August 28, 1942

The sky was clear and blue today. The hills and mountains around the camp were sharply defined in the clear autumn air. I gazed into the distance and images came to mind: my wife and child in Vancouver, the mountains and rivers of my native country. How are they now? I felt an energy coming from within. It is an energy to keep me afloat in the big whirlpool of the war. My eyes filled with tears.

Several letters were returned again today. It is a strange thing. I'm afraid that the postcard which I sent yesterday may come back tomorrow. I washed a shirt. At night as I looked through photographs of a movie magazine. I fell asleep.

August 29, 1942

It was cloudy but warm. It has been so cool and damp lately that it felt warm today. We had a meeting to discuss Nisei citizenship and nationality. Both groups have many good points so we must think very carefully before we decide anything. I wonder which group has the key to their future happiness. To which group does the uncertainty of the future belong?

August 30, 1942

In the morning the camp was covered by fog. The new Japanese who were supposed to arrive at eleven thirty actually arrived around two o'clock. There are forty-six of them, some of whom I know. When they arrived we were in the middle of a meeting to debate the citizenship issue. In the beginning only the Issei met. Later the Issei met with the Nisei Mass Evacuation Group and asked about the problem of giving up citizenship. We had to cut the meeting short because it was already supper time.

After supper we decided that since the matter is very important, four representatives would continue to elicit opinions from the Issei and I was one of the four. We asked the group insisting on rejection of citizenship to proceed carefully and thoughtfully with any decisions. We promised them that we are not taking this matter lightly and would make sure that their opinions were being taken into consideration in finding a solution. The solution would have to satisfy and benefit every compatriot. The Group were set in their opinions and were not willing to change.

August 31, 1942

The present director and his replacement inspected the camp . . . Everybody is hoping that the new director will be a good man. Our camp life depends so much on what kind of person he is . . .

After supper we reported to the Nisei Mass Evacuation Group about yesterday's meetings. I feel that I have done my best. Now I can only hope that the Nisei will find their own solutions.

September 5, 1942

Clear and sunny. It was a peaceful day with seagulls flying in the clear sky.

Twenty-two people were chosen by the authorities to be sent to Japan. The announcement caused pandemonium. Among those who were chosen, some were slightly confused, and some were angry because they heard that they cannot take children over seventeen years of age. I wondered when I would be able to go back to Japan. I am not optimistic.

September 10, 1942

Clear & high temperatures. Around ten o'clock a telegram from Ottawa reached us giving another list of names of Japanese to be deported. I was surprised to find my name on it. I signed without thinking. It is not clear as to when we will depart or what we will need. Former Japanese language school teachers were included in the list. Today is like a teacher's day. All day people greet me with congratulations which made me uncomfortable. I have been feeling guilty and sorry to accept an exchange leaving the Nisei behind. I have been bothered by this thought but I think the time has come to overcome my misgivings.

September 15, 1942

Heavy clouds. Around nine-thirty they summoned S.-san and took him to the exchange ship. But he soon came back. It turned out that he had to wait until tomorrow. The whole camp was buzzing. Everybody is excited and trying to guess who the next person will be.

The seven people who had been detained after the Petawawa incident were set to come back, so we hurriedly set up beds. After supper we went out and saw them approaching the foot of the hill. Everybody must be happy to see them again. We shook hands in the dining room.

September 16, 1942

Cloudy. It was cold in the morning. S.-san left the camp and got on the train after twelve o'clock. We heard the news that seven people including the Nippon Club members are going to Japan. People were very upset and cursed the seven as having connived their way into being exchanged.[22]

October 1, 1942

Clear and sunny. I just finished reading the 600-page biography of Inazo Nitobe. Quietly I kept on thinking about Nitobe's idealism. I wondered in this time of World War what kind of suggestions his internationalism could have given to us.[23]

Our camp leader received a telegram from Charlie Tanaka that said: "The Japanese government is in the middle of making a list of people to be exchanged." It also informed us that the Spanish consul is advising us not to be too optimistic about the POW exchange.

October 10, 1942

We met with the Spanish consul concerning the suspicious death of Mr. T. but he didn't have any information. Also nothing was said about the other questions we had asked. Does the "protecting" country not mean anything? Every one of his visits ends in disappointment.

October 13, 1942

Clear & sunny. First time in a long time I played Go. In the afternoon an officer came from Ottawa to meet with dozens of Nisei and some Issei who had been applying for release from the camp. The details are not clear but it is said that in the next ten days they are going to decide on their future. As the rumours of exchanges subside the new talk is about releases. Again the camp is filled with a strange excitement and energy.

Received a letter from my wife. This is the first one since the beginning of September. She hadn't written because she had been expecting to leave for Japan but now she has finally given up hope.

October 14, 1942

There was the election of the hut leader and I almost won but I insisted on declining until a second candidate came forward. Thus I am assured a bit of freedom.

October 15, 1942

School began and I taught at the sixth grade level in the morning.

October 16, 1942

Good weather continues. I took a German language class but with my bad memory I'm not optimistic. I also attended an English class. I had an extremely busy day.

October 19, 1942

I thought about Reika and what kind of a life she must be leading. I can imagine her in a red coat and I wonder how much she must have grown since those days.

At a party somebody used an expression which offended the Citizenship Rejection group and they in turn lodged a protest. Concerning this incident I was asked to become a mediator. So until the evening roll call I met with both groups to find out what everybody wanted.

October 20, 1942

There were strong winds blowing dust which made for an unpleasant day. Concerning yesterday's problem I had to run around mediating between the different groups but I couldn't come up with any kind of agreement that would satisfy either group. So finally there was nothing left to do but to get them together to talk among themselves. But some people worry that they might fight over the way they are to meet and talk, but what else can you do? This is a problem between man and man and there must be a solution. It looks very bleak but I'm not pessimistic.

October 21, 1942

I was summoned to the dining hall to attend the meeting concerning the same incident. After they reached an agreement, I was asked to make a speech as a mediator.

A registered letter arrived from my wife. Besides her report on family finances, she says that going to Japan does not seem possible anymore.

October 29, 1942

The temperature went up and the snow began to melt. I received a telegram from my wife reporting her departure to Slocan. The departure was supposed to be yesterday so she must have arrived in Slocan by today. My sight was darkened as I tried to imagine Yoshiko and Reika being herded out of Vancouver. But on the other hand now I feel completely cleansed of Vancouver. I pray for their health and good life in Slocan.

November 1, 1942

Overcast. The temperature is still high. I have a feeling that on Sundays I must relax, so I just spend the day lazily playing Go and resting. Since this morning I feel good. It's probably because we are expecting a Japanese meal with green tea that was received from the Japanese Red Cross. With that to come I went for a walk and exercised before supper to make myself hungry. How petty to be excited about such a small luxury.

Finally supper time came. Just the smell of the tea made me want to cry for joy. "Dear Compatriots in my country, please know that your kindness reached across the ocean and is making us Japanese tearful with happiness. Please forgive us, who spend empty days in POW camps without being able to contribute anything to you." Thus I prayed to the tea. Probably every internee shared my appreciation.

November 2, 1942

Temperature dropped a bit. Got a letter from my wife. This was the last letter before her departure from Vancouver. She said that she cried when she wrote it.

November 3, 1942

Temperature plummeted to six below zero this morning. It got so cold that I couldn't sleep. Today is *Meiji-setsu*, the birthday of the late Meiji emperor, which I used to celebrate when he was still alive. I feel very nostalgic. The weather turned out clear and sunny, a perfect day. And today we enjoyed the victorious progress of our Imperial country. As we welcome this occasion the mind of the Japanese inevitably feels uplifted.

After the worship ceremony there were entertainments but I left just after the ceremony. All day I enjoyed warm thoughts towards the late great emperor of Meiji.

November 4, 1942

All day there were terrible winds. Each time I go to the dining hall I am almost blown off my feet. Went to see a funny movie; won only once in *Go*; practised *shakuhachi*; and reviewed my German lesson. After evening roll call the wind became so strong that the barracks began creaking and swaying back and forth. The battle in the Solomon Islands continues. The airport is said to have been occupied by the Americans.

November 5, 1942

Cold. Received gifts from Yoshiko. Immensely thankful. How precious she is to me.

We had a discussion about the Nisei problem. This is an inevitable problem which we have to face, now that relocation of the families have been completed. To me this is such a serious and difficult problem, so I refrained from giving my opinion. I understand that to ask the young people for the same kind of determination as ours is not fair.

November 7, 1942

At breakfast we got small apples, which I must say is rare.

Today's war reports say that the Axis was defeated both in Libya and on the Russian front.

November 9, 1942

In the morning sleet changed into snow, so it was terribly depressing weather all day. Those who had been applying for release are finally leaving. I wonder what their feelings are. My friend S.-san is one of the twenty-eight who is going. As we have been together in camp for a long time, I too feel very emotional about all of this . . . Anyhow, I'm happy for him who is finally going to be united with his family.

I shook his hand and bade him farewell. I wanted to see them off but it was cold and snowing so I stayed in.

November 16, 1942

The Axis defeat in North Africa is coming to a tragic end.

November 17, 1942

I hear that there are conflicting arguments about release. After all, it's left up to each person's belief. There is news that a decisive naval battle is to be fought soon between Japan and the United States.

November 19, 1942

The temperature went up again. I finally received my wife's first letter from Slocan. I can only imagine the very uncomfortable life there. They only have candlelight, so I can picture what the rest of their life is like. Do the authorities still insist that this is to protect Japanese Canadians? Wouldn't it be better under the banner of "persecution." Even in wartime, how can they justify treating civilians and especially women and children, with such cruelty? When the big Japanese victory comes, the people doing this will have to answer for their actions.

Reika's letter was enclosed. I was so surprised to see how good her handwriting is. The way the letters lined up was very impressive. It was also the first time that my wife's letter was cut up by the censors. I am curious to know which words they deemed as dangerous.

December 7, 1942

Clear. This is the anniversary of the beginning of the war between Japan, Britain and the United States. Our new fate began exactly a year ago today, and also that day Japan chose its new destiny. In our proud 2,600 years of history this was the day that changed the face of our nation. It is the day when our great nation asserted itself against the white race. We Japanese who are overseas, have been isolated in enemy countries

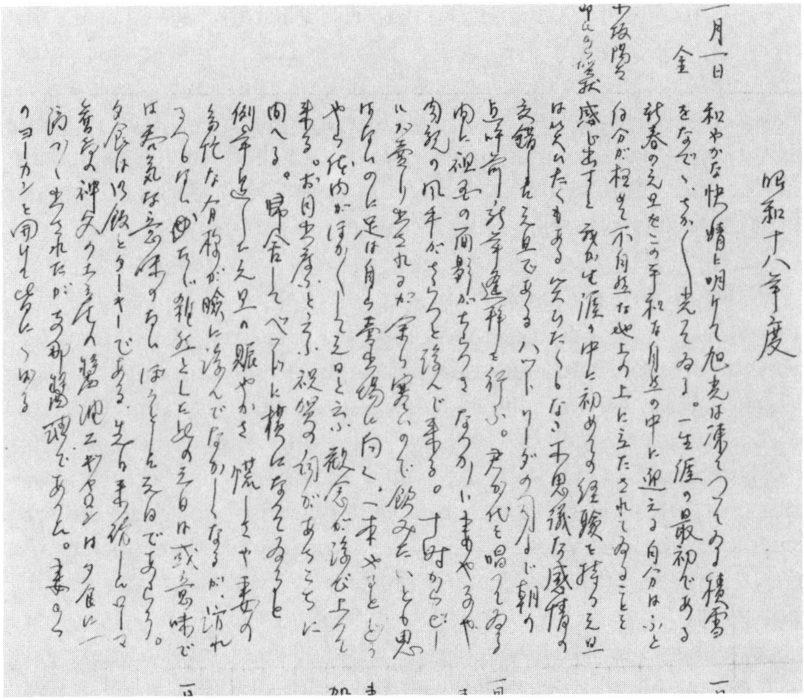

A page from Koichiro Miyazaki's diary, written while in Angler prison camp, dated Showa 18 or Friday, January 1, 1943.

and our families are scattered. But despite our hardships we believe that everything is for our native country's future. This faith keeps me going. I believe that I am not the only one filled with confidence. I sent a short note to my wife with my feeling on this important day. After morning role call we had one minute of silence and then sang Kimigayo, our national anthem. Our hut leader, Mr. I. made a short speech. I wonder what my eighty-one fellow hut members were thinking and feeling.

December 15, 1942

It was clear and sunny today with high temperatures. The rumour was confirmed by the announcement that eighty-eight people were being released. Many of those who had been arrested just after the Pearl Harbour attack are included in the release group. Among them are Ariga and Iwashita.[24] F., whose bed was next to me, is going as well. I will miss him. I imagine those who believe in liberalism must have suffered much over the past year but I have no sympathy for their liberalism. I even despise it. While hating their philosophy I still feel attached to the individuals.

I even hated to shake hands with some of them but I actually gave each person a kind word of farewell and shook their hands. Then I saw them off at the gate.

December 25, 1942

Christmas day. My first Christmas as a prisoner. It is a beautiful day and the temperature is high. Although the weather is good we don't have anything special to do. All we can do is to reflect on our past memories of Christmas. Around three o'clock beer was sold. You could only buy one bottle. Not that ordinarily I would want more beer but just the limitation makes me crave more. At night I opened a package of chocolate and shared it with my friends.

December 27, 1942

It got cold. I received a handmade Christmas card from Reika.

January 1, 1943

The New Year began with a mild and fine day. The snow sparkled in the sunshine. I thought, this might be my first New Year's Day spent in such a peaceful and natural environment; then the next moment I realized how unnatural it is for me to be here during the war. I felt like laughing yet I didn't want to laugh. It is a strange New Year with strangely mixed-up feelings. Under the hut leader's orders we worshipped the Emperor before roll call while singing the Japanese national anthem. Images of my country, my family, and my wife and child passed before me. Beer was sold at 10:00. It's so cold that I didn't feel like drinking, yet my legs carried me there. One bottle managed to make me feel warmer and began to put me in a New Year's mood. People greeted one another: Omedeto, Happy New Year. I returned to the hut and lay down on the bed. I could not stop thinking about the cheerful and hectic atmosphere of past New Year's and of busily preparing for the occasion. It made me feel nostalgic. Without visitors and with nothing to do the day is meaningless, so I just relaxed without thinking about anything.

January 10, 1943

Overcast. The temperature is high. It was my turn to be in charge of the washroom until eleven o'clock. The carpenter M.-san made geta, a pair of wooden clogs. The ones I made myself in Petawawa had worn out. As I threw the old ones into the stove I felt bad about throwing them away. The fact that I am even moved by this kind of thing stunned me. After all I lived with these clogs for eight months. I felt lazy and low-spirited all day.

After supper I talked with F. and A. about how badly we treat our wives. Although the conversation was on a light note, in my mind it was very serious. I regretted ever being insensitive towards my wife.

January 18, 1943

Last night I could not sleep very well because of the cold. I got up to find out that there were also a lot of people who could not sleep well. Here and there people were grumbling about the cold. As we went out for breakfast, we really felt the temperature. Because of the cold I had a pain in the back of my head and my teeth were freezing. I could not help but run to get to the dining hall. The thermometer read forty below.

January 23, 1943

Clear and sunny. The temperature is high. After roll call there were elections for hut leaders. My bunkmates decided that it was now my turn. I had no interest in the job so I tried to decline. But since I refused the job once before there was nothing I could do but accept. It means that I will have to suspend my studies. Too bad.

February 1, 1943

Today was *Koa-hoko-bi*, Asian Prosperity Service Day, and after roll call we had a moment of silence with the rest of my hut members. Rumours are going around that there was a riot in the Japanese relocation camp in Tashme. One person died, five seriously injured and forty other slightly injured. But I don't know whether these rumours are true or not.[25]

February 22, 1943

Clear and sunny.
A letter arrived from my wife which was dated February 4th. There is no particular news but she says she will continue to live day by day.

> In the wake of the pen
> I long for her
> Spring is still young

February 25, 1943

The temperature dropped to twenty-five below. I received a Valentine chocolate from Reika. I feel happier than usual.

> Snowy day
> Spread eagled
> Prisoners nap

March 3, 1943

Yesterday was sixty below but today it is slightly warmer. But still it is no higher than thirty below. Today is *momo-no-sekku* (Girls' Day).[26] But in this severe cold and snow just to think of the word *momo-no-sekku* is upsetting. I recalled with nostalgia that Reika, with the help of her mother, spent one week preparing for the celebration. It is sad to imagine how lonely my family are feeling today.

March 7, 1943

Sunday. A fateful day. I was arrested one year ago today. The memory of my wife and daughter seeing me off through the drizzling rain is with me as if it had happened yesterday. I think that in Slocan my wife will be going through the same thing. After three o'clock I asked the group of thirteen who were together in the Immigration Building in

Vancouver with me, to gather together. With beer and instant *shiruko* [sweet bean desert] we had a party and shared the past.

March 14, 1943

It's a little colder. In an American magazine I read an article called, "Black Brain Trusts." It's about an organization of twenty-five black people challenging the White House with eight demands. They say that if the U.S. argues that this war is for freedom, then they are also determined to fight for their own freedom. Very interesting. According to the article there are thirteen million black people in the U.S.

I attended the hut leader meeting at two o'clock. Supper was a treat of curry with rice.

March 21, 1943

Sunday. There are so many sick people here. The hospital is full. I hope we don't have a flu or cold epidemic. At two o'clock and we had a memorial ceremony for H. who died on the eighth in the hospital. We held the ceremony in the recreation hall. As I listen a close friend of H.'s giving the eulogy, I couldn't stop the tears from flowing. It was a strange thing, I didn't know what was happening to me. I imagined that H.'s parents must be in Japan praying for his safety and they don't even know what has happened to him.

Melting snow drips
In the quiet afternoon
Memorial service

March 26, 1943

Clear and sunny. Since early this morning it has been so cold that I could not sleep. As I got up, I heard somebody complaining loudly. The troublemaker of the hut is R. who was almost shouting and it became clear that he was criticizing me as the hut leader. When I began to argue with him he finally stopped. It was tense and it looked like something might develop but then it ended as quickly as it had begun. Around the time we did our exercises, the wind began to blow.

Today, four more people were released. Mr. M. and his son were included in the release. Mr. M. used to be one of the most militant, hard-liners but look what happened. That's usually how it goes.

I sent a letter to my wife. I mentioned the importance of volunteer work in the community and how lucky we were to have Reika as our child.

April 6, 1943

Warm. Spring-like day. I translated an English thesis about the containment of China. Doctor N., who is a military surgeon, was at the camp performing surgery. He asked my Japanese friend, Doctor H. to assist him. During the surgery the military Doctor said the following to H.:

"It's hard to say when the war will end and in what way. However one thing is certain, the Allies will win. The Japanese in Canada will all be deported, except those loyal to Canada. For the Nisei there wouldn't be a place in Japan so they should begin studying Spanish or some other such language, to be ready for South America."

Doctor H. was seething while he told me of this.

According to another friend of mine, a soldier asked him why he didn't go out and work. So my friend answered that even if he wanted to the only thing that the authorities let us do is clear land. The soldier responded that it was a shame for Canada to put good Japanese people into such a place. The soldier continued: "I was also in the German POW camps but they were terrible. They would spit on you or try and be rough with you. When I was moved to Angler my colleagues said that I was lucky and now I know what they meant." Then he discreetly gave my friend some candy and asked whether my friend wanted to drink a beer. My friend declined.

April 27, 1943

My friend Doctor H. was released.

April 29, 1943

It is the happy occasion of the Emperor's birthday. At 7:40 there was a worship ceremony. I don't know why, but there was no emotion like last year at Petawawa. Is it because of the surrounding landscape? I received a letter from my wife postmarked April 17. After considering various aspects, she says she is now negotiating with the B.C. Security Commission for permission to move to Toronto and build a life there. She says this may happen by the end of this month. This was unexpected news to me and surprised me. I wonder what made her do that? She says she decided alone because it is almost impossible for me to understand her feelings. I cannot help wondering: is it in order to escape the pain of her routine life, for our child's education, for my sake, or to earn her living? I can imagine that she wants to expand her options in a completely new environment, but before I encourage her I tend to worry about her health and the hardships that she will have to go through. On the other hand I feel I should trust her strength and fighting spirit. I read the letter over and over again and contemplated it all afternoon and evening, anxious and not knowing what to do. I can't send a telegram, and a letter with my opinions will be too late. I feel frustrated. But what can I do except write a letter anyway?

May 1, 1943

May has arrived. But today we don't see the bright sun of May. Here in Angler it is still cold and the sky looks dark and overcast like the colour of lead.

This day last year, we had a hunger strike at the Petawawa camp. The tense atmosphere of those days is no longer evident. In the afternoon, instead of going to the movie I remained completely idle. It was quiet and a perfect time to lie back and remember my wife and daughter. I washed a pair of my pants but they will not dry within the day.

May 27, 1943

Today is Japanese Navy Memorial day. The camp is shrouded in a white fog. Before roll call there was a simple ceremony. In fact it was so simple that I wouldn't even call it a ceremony.

I continued with translation. Mr. S. who has the bunk near me and who is also my teacher of shakuhachi flute was released along with some others.

July 1, 1943

Dominion Day. Already July. How fast time goes. I feel that autumn is just around the corner.

This day last year the camp was in turmoil and I can still hear clearly the sounds of gunshots in the night. After supper those who were detained in that incident got together and cooked sukiyaki dinner and invited four of us to share memories of the past.

July 11, 1943

Clear and sunny. Sunday. There was an athletic meet to commemorate the sixth anniversary of the China Incident. The first thing one does at

a commemoration is to observe a minute of silence in order to feel
gratitude but I found it in poor taste to march around in a party-like
atmosphere. I entered the relay race and our team was running second
before I ran, but because I fell our team ended up placing last. I felt
sorry but at the same time I was shocked to discover how my physical
condition deteriorated. My head ran ahead of me and my body wouldn't
follow and as a result I fell twice. I couldn't believe it.

July 19, 1943

I received Yoshiko's twenty-second letter today. As she has had to give
up hope of going back to Japan she is depressed and has lost much of
her ambition to go on. I can always use the word "fate" but what could
it do or mean for her. I hate to end up hurting her by trying to console
her. It was such a depressing day that I almost felt physically ill.

July 21, 1943

This day last year I came here from Petawawa. I look back at all the
uneventful and mundane days. One could say that our lives became
settled but more accurately our lives withered and became empty. These
days we move without going anywhere. We just placidly follow the
routine. I studied a bit but it's far from satisfying. While I was away my
family was taken to a ghost town. At least I am not sick and have managed
to survive. It is frightening to think that I must continue this monotonous
life for many more years. There must be some changes in this coming
year. I expect that the number of prisoners will be greatly reduced.
Already more than two hundred people have left. This trend will
probably continue and I expect some big changes in the war itself. Like
everybody I do hope that the end of the War will come soon but I must
be ready for a long and continuous war. I must trim the wasteful and
unnecessary from my life and make the days more meaningful.

July 27, 1943

Front page newspaper headlines reported that Mussolini has fallen from
power. We cannot confirm if this is true or not but considering the
situation of the Italian military it appears to be true. This may be a sign
that Italy has been defeated. If so it will no doubt be a source of worry
for the Axis.

July 28, 1943

The fall of Mussolini seems to be a fact. According to the reports the fate of Italy will be decided by the end of the week.

July 30, 1943

I went to work on the top of a hill and in the gorge there are hundreds of flowers in bloom. It was a nice day and I felt good. When I returned my wife's letter was waiting for me. I really don't know why she continues to feel so depressed. Her letter betrays a desperate mind. She declares that she will stop writing to me, but during wartime what else can we do? We must look around and notice that there are many people also suffering. When we think about our whole life, this can be seen as just a small thing. Also when we think about the whole history of the Japanese nation, it is stupid to be so emotional. As I ponder all this I begin to feel depressed. I don't want to write to her anymore either.

August 13, 1943

From a friend I received socks and toothpowder which are very difficult to get here. I was very happy.

I read Canadian history and I'm learning a lot. I found out how Canada was built over four centuries by sacrificing native Indians. I was surprised that even in Canada there have been so many wars and struggles. That makes the theory of a democratic and peaceful Canada look hypocritical.

September 10, 1943

It became clear that Italy surrendered unconditionally. As I read about the tragic fall of the Italian nation I remembered those ambitious, vain words of Mussolini. Now I only hope that the Germans and Japanese can gather up enough spirit to fight on.

September 11, 1943

Yesterday I forgot to bring in a pot of flowers from outside and during the night there was frost and now they are darkened and withered. So I was quite sad before I even received my wife's letter. I opened it and immediately noticed that it was very short and the handwriting was rough (expressing her total despair). She declares that she is going to Eastern Canada. On the one hand I felt I didn't care, but I also felt sad to see her struggling and so unhappy.

October 29, 1943

Clear and sunny. I received a letter from my wife that she wrote on September 28th, on the train on her way to Eastern Canada. So just a month ago my wife and daughter were passing very near here without knowing I was close by. She wants to buy a nice doll for Reika with the money she is going to earn working.

I was awakened by some people who wanted me to go to the movies. Still half asleep I followed them. Part of the movie featured the Chicago Opera and another Italian Opera. I was very happy to hear the beautiful voices of the world's greatest singers. However, while I was enjoying this treat most of the audience who had never heard or seen real opera before were either bored, laughing at it, or making stupid remarks. I had never seen such a noisy audience. As I sat there I began to feel disgusted with my fellow Japanese and I wondered whether the bad taste that remained about my own people will quickly disappear.

November 6, 1943

The snow storm ended and the day became clear. Now I can see the silhouette of people walking outside. I had nothing to do.

Re-election of the hut leader. I felt sympathy for the candidates as they were booed and heckled, but what can I do with this collection of misfits? I wrote a card to Reika asking her to overcome the loneliness, help Mama and be good. It was the first mail that I sent to Montreal.

November 15, 1943

When I awoke at six-thirty the temperature was minus eight. It was the first time this season that the temperature has been below zero. I received a second letter from Montreal dated October 30. As I read it I felt very sorry for Yoshiko and tears welled up into my eyes. She finally found a job as a live-in housemaid in a *keto* house.[27] Thousands of miles away from home, she is now trying to earn a living and raise our child in an unknown land. It is a depressing thought that she who was brought up in a good family is now working like a slave without even being able to understand the language well. While I am wasting time in a place like this she is working hard from morning to night trying to keep her tears inside. I can't stand it. How far do we have to go along this dark road? . . . But I cannot give up my principles, and probably she too will maintain her own determination. I can't bear the fact that I am powerless to lessen her suffering. I toss and turn in bed without being able to sleep.

I wonder how my daughter is reacting to such a life? It is a relief to hear that she has entered a school. She might be brought up in real *keto*-style but nothing can be done. For now I can only pray that both parents and child will live through these hard days in good health until the day when we will be reunited.

December 1, 1943

This is the second December spent in an internment camp. I am watching the white snowflakes dancing outside. Even that makes me feel helpless. I eat, sleep, get up and simply pray for the safety of my wife and child and for Japan's victory. I know that this is my fate and the path that I have chosen. Knowing that I still feel split and dissatisfied. I simply wish to live silently without complaints but sometimes I cannot help complaining.

Received a letter from Yoshiko filled with pessimism.

December 31, 1943

A clear sky and the temperature is high. This is the last day of 1943. Many changes occurred in my life this year. Since she has given up hope about going back to Japan by POW exchanges, my wife has become depressed and pessimistic. Her last ray of hope is gone. Since August, most of her letters have been filled with hateful words. She left a ghost town, travelled more than a thousand miles to Montreal to end up as a housemaid. How ironic that she, who grew up spoiled in a good family, became a maid. It is a sad story, yet this too is one phase of our life. I have been trying with all my might to console her. I am a short-tempered person but I tried hard to control myself to continue writing to her. And I feel that it was the wind of the time that drove me to do so. I have been reading news articles that report how the Allies are winning as demonstrated by Italy's surrender. That only adds to the confusion I feel. Even when I discount the Allied propaganda, it's still very hard to see the light in this war. As the saying goes, the sun is setting and there's still a long way to go along the road. I also have to admit that I could not accomplish my studies as I had planned. I started with lots of energy and determination but it didn't last too long. I know how stupid it is to waste time in such a place and I feel unhappy with myself for not making an effort to change. But another year has come to an end. Time does not wait. A profound truth.

January 1, 1944

Woke up at seven. After washing I went out and gazed towards the east, praying for the best for my beloved country. And as I was praying for the health of my family my eyes became hot with tears. I was alone in the darkness. I stood silently with my eyes closed and my head hanging down as images of the landscape of my country and of my wife and child struggling in Montreal came to my mind. Unwittingly, I stumbled backwards and heard the snow collapsing under my feet.

January 29, 1944

The Japanese camp leader offered his resignation so we all voted whether to accept his resignation offer or not. Our barracks, 4A, cast 47 votes for accepting his resignation and 19 against. I was upset about this terrible impoliteness. I translated part of a *Reader's Digest* article.

March 2, 1944

Snowflakes swirled around silently today. The temperature rose to 34. As I sat at the desk reading and then thinking about March, I suddenly felt nostalgic. I corrected one of my student's translations. Britain announced that it had wiped out the Japanese on the Burmese front. But the Japanese side insists that they inflicted a crucial blow to the British forces. How complex wartime reports are.

March 7, 1944

Two years ago today I was detained at the Immigration Building. I wonder what significance that day is going to have in the history of my life. My memory of that day is still very vivid: my determination to sacrifice my own freedom and family life for the love of my country and the pride of my people.

The war has smashed our life completely to pieces. Not only have my wife and I changed, but we are splitting farther apart day by day. Only the mind of our child is growing straight and pure. I wonder how long this dark tunnel will go on. Will the conclusion of the war bring the end of this dark tunnel into sight, I wonder.

March 29, 1944

In the afternoon a severe snow storm began. The barracks swayed back and forth in the driving wind. Churchill's radio speech that I was looking forward to hearing turned out to be very ordinary. It was a show to trick the enemy.

March 30, 1944

The storm stopped. I translated Courier magazine and then in the evening I wrote a birthday letter to my daughter.

May 28, 1944

We held a ceremony commemorating Japanese Navy memorial day in the afternoon. The ceremony itself was extremely simple. The entertainments were so bad and tasteless that I had to leave.

June 22, 1944

News reports say that a major naval battle near Saipan Island will soon occur. A fly is buzzing desperately around in the window trying to get out. It's comic, yet it's sad. How can I laugh at it when I compare myself to it? My case is even worse. The fly is only here accidentally. I washed some shirts.

July 7, 1944

Anniversary of the China Incident. Seven years seems such a long time ago but as long as we are Japanese we should keep on marking this day. But many people are completely forgetful; it's not only that they don't give a minute of silence, they openly enjoy gambling as usual. This is very hard to bear.

It turned out that the American landing at Ogasawara Islands turned out to be a groundless rumour.

July 18, 1944

I spent all day feeling bad because of the heavy pain in my leg where I was bitten by an insect yesterday. At dusk a heavy rain started with hail and thunder. The lightning flashing outside intermittently lit up the dark room. I leaned against the desk and stared out through the window in silence. I felt a sudden urge to scream. It seems everything will be destroyed. No letter again.

July 19, 1944

A terrible pain in my leg. I didn't feel like doing anything.

July 20, 1944

News reports say that Prime Minister Tojo resigned to assume responsibility for the defeat in the Saipan battle. The death toll was reported. The state of the war seems to be very depressing for us.

July 21, 1944

The death of Hitler in an explosion was reported.

July 22, 1944

More ominous news for the Axis forces. I hope that as long as the people's minds are close to the government, Japan cannot be as shaken as the newspapers report. I'm still waiting for my wife's letter in vain. I could not study at all today.

July 23, 1944

I couldn't do anything.

July 24, 1944

Two letters from Dr. H. As I received them I knew they were going to contain bad news. I was right. My wife is in critical condition. She is too weak to be operated on. I felt as if everything had been lost in blackness. My child who has just come out of the hospital is now deprived of her mother and has been taken into somebody's care. My wife who has been desperately fighting since the beginning of the war, is finally failing. I am moved by Dr. H. earnestly urging me to come out and for the first time I have begun to consider asking for a never-dreamed-of release. After discussing it with Mr. M. I decided to swallow my pride and tears and appeal for release. I wonder when destiny will stop playing with us like puppets? Fine. I'm just going to fight to the end.

The newspaper tells of the turmoil in Germany and the American landing on the island of Guam. Today everything seems to be filled with darkness. I wrote to Reika and to Dr. H.

July 25, 1944

Headache today. I remained motionless in bed. I had visions of my wife and child and couldn't stop the tears from falling.

July 29, 1944

Because my release might take some time I sent a telegram to Dr. H. asking him, in case of emergency, to please go ahead with the operation.

T W O L E T T E R S

[To his wife]

March 6, 1944

Dear Yoshiko,

I read your letter of February 4. You say that by reading my letter of January 20 you realized that we would never be able to agree. I am the one who should be blamed for that so I do not know what to say. I just feel very sorry for you. Maybe I should be regretting my past decisions that deserve your anger, but what's done is done. What can I do except pray for your health and our child's well-being? I have been listening to your hateful, angry words since last summer, although it was not easy. But, as you said in your last letter, even if you stop writing for good it would not make my life easier nor lessen my responsibility. You have asked me why we came to Canada in the first place. My answer would only make you angrier. I doubt that words of regret about the past would be able to give you happiness. I will just torment myself for having made you so unhappy and bear the pain as well. So please do not be afraid to disagree with me. Do not hesitate to say what you want to say. I think I have become able to listen to you with a humble heart. You say that our daughter is a good child. Even discounting perhaps some wishful thinking, I'm very thankful for it. I believe it's all thanks to you. Please continue your efforts.

Take care.

[To his daughter]

March 31, 1944

Dear Reika,

You haven't forgotten Japanese, have you? When you see a character that you have forgotten, ask Mama to read it. Today it is your birthday. How old are you now? Nine, aren't you? It's a beautiful day today. The snowflakes are sparkling as if they are celebrating your birthday. Your daddy cannot give you any present for your birthday. I hope you forgive me for that. But I heard from your mother that she wants to have a birthday party for you at Mrs. K.'s or somewhere. So I hope by now you will be enjoying your birthday cake. This is your third birthday without daddy. But you must be happy since your Mama is always with you. Please do not catch a cold, stay in good health and study hard. Be good to your Mama and grow big.

Love,

Daddy.

NOTES

1. The "office" refers to the Japanese-language newspaper that the author worked for.

2. The Thesis On Japanese Spirit and The History of the National Flag respectively.

3. The China Incident refers to the beginning of open warfare between Japan and China following the Japanese invasion in 1937.

4. The Japanese language school where the author was the principal.

5. The "committee" refers to the Japanese liaison committee whose members were appointed by the government's standing committee, an advisory body created several months before Pearl Harbour. The "boss" and also the "King" refers to the gambling boss Etsuji Morii who exercised a strong influence in the pre-war Japanese community in British Columbia. The authorities repeatedly made use of his power to control the community.

6. Mitsuru Shinpo, Kanada Nihonjin Imin Monogatari (Tokyo: Tsukiji-shokan, 1986), 172-73. The Nisei, or the children of the immigrants who were born in Canada, were automatically Canadian citizens. According to the census data in 1941, about 60% of the population were Nisei and 15% naturalized Issei, therefore three-quarters of the Japanese-Canadian population were Canadian citizens. The rest were called 'nationals' or Japanese citizens. Many of them were refused naturalization although they wanted to be citizens. The anti-Japanese campaign created a vicious circle which pushed the Issei toward Japanese nationalism.

7. Among those who were arrested just after the outbreak of the Pacific War were many individuals connected with Japanese language schools. Even before the War the schools were seen as a hotbed of Japanese nationalism and were often targets of anti-Japanese propaganda.

8. First the Morii group advocated the government's "partial evacuation" policy, believing that the Japanese "nationals" could save the rest of the Japanese Canadians from forced removal by "sacrificing" themselves and going to road camps. When the Canadian government, following similar action in the United States, decided on February 26 to opt for total evacuation, the Morii group lost credibility in the Japanese Canadian community. At the same time, those who gambled on Canadian democracy and British "fair play," were deflated.

9. From 8 March to 31 March 1942, the dates in the diary were originally written as occurring in July. Later Miyazaki changed them to March, indicating that he was trying to disguise his documents in case they fell into the wrong hands.

10. Although some thought the red circle represented a crude version of the Japanese flag, it was, in fact, more like a target.

11. Chiyokichi Ariga, Rokki no Yuwaku (The Temptation of the Rockies) (Tokyo: Rikkyo Elementary School 1952), 104-105. The arrival of the thirteen Japanese,

including Miyazaki, is described in this book: "Eleven-twenty a.m. thirteen new Japanese arrived to join us. I don't know what is the cause of their detention, but whatever the causes of their detention, they were acting like heros." Ariga, a former school principal who was among the thirty-eight people who had been detained earlier in the POW camp observed contrasts in the attitudes between the group of thirty-eight and the group of thirteen new arrivals: "Those thirteen believed that not working is the right of the POW and refused to any kind of labour. There was nothing we could do. They demanded an interview with Lieutenant Colonel Watson . . . Watson was a career officer and was not a flexible man. He said, 'My responsibility is over when I've given you your rice and pickles. You should be thankful to be able to eat, just like soldiers. Yes, you are obligated to work. So what!' The group of thirteen, though aggressive, were no match for Lieutenant Colonel Watson, and ended up agreeing to work starting the next day . . . The argument of the group of thirteen slowly managed to disturb the unity of the group of thirty-eight to the point where the Committee leader Iwashita had to resign."

12. Refers to diaries which recorded events prior to Miyazaki's detention. The author re-wrote some of the censored diaries, parts of which appear in Miyazaki's Memoir section in this book.

13. Boys' Day is celebrated with special dolls representing folk heroes, banners, and fish streamers.

14. Oku no hosomichi is a poetic journal written by the great seventeenth century poet Basho Matsuo, creator of haiku poetry.

15. Keto is a derogatory word for white people, literally meaning "hairy stranger."

16. "Gang" probably refers to the Morii gang in Vancouver, British Columbia.

17. Ken Adachi, The Enemy That Never Was: A History of the Japanese Canadians (Toronto: McClelland and Stewart, 1976), 237. "Instead of selecting Canadian-born representatives, who might have been most ready to co-operate as a test of the 'loyalty,' Security Commission Chairman Austin Taylor chose Morii, along with two fellow Issei, Arthur Nishiguschi and Ippei Nishio, to form a 'liaison' committee which would act as an intermediary between the Japanese community and the government agency. Morii was well-known to the RCMP, for he had worked with them during the recent investigation of illegal immigration. But clearly, Morii was not a man who enjoyed the confidence of the Japanese community in terms of his integrity, objectivity or personality."

18. See 28 April 1942.

19. The Nisei Mass Evacuation Group was a semi-underground movement among the Nisei who were against the government policy of breaking-up families by sending the men away to camps. Many Nisei of the group ended up in the Petawawa and Angler POW camps.

20. When a group of Nisei prepared to follow the urging of the government

to relocate to the East, hard-line Nisei attempted to physically prevent them from doing so. In the struggle that ensued, alarmed camp guards began to shoot, but no one was injured.

21. *Obon* is the summer festival when the ancestral spirits are welcomed back to this world.

22. The Nippon Club was an organization of mainly successful business people in the pre-war Vancouver Japanese community. It seems that the seven people referred to in this diary entry are perceived by the author and his compatriots as having cooperated with the British Columbia authorities.

23. Inazio Nitobe was a well-known intellectual who was seen as a bridge between Japan and the West.

24. Chiyokichi Ariga, *Rokki no Yuwaku* (Tokyo: Rikkyo Elementary School).

25. This rumour of a riot with many casualties turned out to be false.

26. Girls' Day is represented by the symbol of the *momo*, peach blossom.

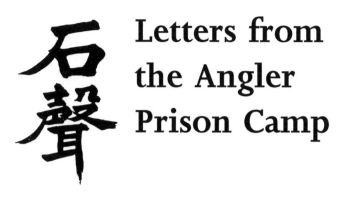

Letters from the Angler Prison Camp

Kensuke Kitagawa

Letters from the Angler Prison Camp

KENSUKE KITAGAWA

Editor's Introduction

Kensuke Kitagawa was born in 1895 in Kumamoto Prefecture, Japan. When he was eighteen years old he came to Canada to work with his father who was a farm labourer on Vancouver Island. In 1926 he returned to Japan to marry a woman from Hiroshima. They settled in Duncan on Vancouver Island where they ran a dry-cleaning business. His wife Kotoma also worked as a seamstress on the side. Kensuke Kitagawa also ran a small taxi business with his brother who owned a grocery store. The taxi service served Japanese immigrant workers who lived in logging camps in the mountains. In the town of Duncan itself there were only seven Japanese-Canadian households. Kitagawa held responsible positions in the local Japanese Association.

Mrs. Kitagawa, widowed since her husband's death in 1974, tells us how it was after the beginning of the Pacific War.

> We spent four months, many days without knowing anything about tomorrow. We secluded ourselves in the darkened house with the windows closed. Since there were not too many Japanese around, we felt surrounded by white people and, in fact, they did watch us carefully. They informed on us to the police, saying for instance, that 'Kitagawa left home in the early evening,' and so on. They would watch from behind curtains.

The notice ordering them to leave within twenty-four hours finally came.

On the twentieth of April we arrived in Hastings Park. It was surrounded by barbed wire. We had to line up in the dining hall, holding a tin place in our hands, wanting to cry from shame. At first I couldn't swallow the food. I was so sad to be there like a beggar while hakujin watched us from outside the fence. But to survive, we had to eat . . .

Among our men, those who were even a bit against the government's policies were sent to POW camps. My husband had a rebellious spirit so he might as well have volunteered to go. At first I had no idea where he was being taken. That was the most anxious time for me. Much later, I began to receive letters. They were all cut up, and full of holes like a strainer.

It is these censored letters, both to herself and others that Mrs. Kitagawa neatly copied in her notebook. Unlike many who could leave the Angler internment camp if they agreed to settle in Eastern Canada, Kensuke Kitagawa chose to remain in the camp until the end of the war. His wife explains:

My husband was a ganbari-ya, a die-hard. His younger brother was in the same camp too but he left because he had kids to take care of. My husband was one of the last hold-outs of the Angler ganbari-ya. He refused to be released.

During the war, however, the ganbari-ya sentiment was not exclusively found at the Angler camp in Ontario. Mrs. Kitagawa, who spent three years in Slocan, tells us:

In Slocan I was thinking that Japan would win. Although we Japanese were forbidden to keep radios, there was always someone who kept one secretly, and underground newsletters would circulate to inform people about the war as it was reported by the Imperial War Bureau in Japan. And also people would say to watch out for the inu, dogs, who would spy on us. So we had to be careful what we said and to whom.

At the end of the war 425 men were still incarcerated in the Ontario POW camps. Even after the war ended with Japan's surrender, Kitagawa

Japanese passport photo of Kensuke Kitagawa.

remained in the group that continued to refuse "to have anything to do with evacuation, relocation and repatriation." In July 1946 he was among the 128 Nisei and Issei men who were shipped to Moose Jaw, Saskatchewan.[1] Mrs. Kitagawa explains:

> When the Angler camp was closed they wanted to move the remaining Japanese men somewhere else, but every province refused to take them, except Saskatchewan. So the last group of *ganbari-ya* were sent to Moose Jaw. They were installed at the small military base. As my husband refused to listen to me, I had settled in Toronto and was renting a room at a friend's place. I wrote to Moose Jaw from Toronto, urging him to come and join me. I said that we could work together again, as husband and wife, just like in the old days.

When she finally arrived in Moose Jaw, Mrs. Kitagawa found her husband already released and setting up a cleaning business. They ended up staying in Moose Jaw until they retired in 1968 and moved to Vancouver. Kensuke Kitagawa died in 1974. His wife kept some of his ashes and recently travelled to Japan to inter them in his native Kumamoto. She says, "I have already asked my niece to take some of my ashes to the same place."

One feature that stands out in the Kitagawa letters is his increasingly passionate devotion to religious faith. From his letters we discover that he encountered a series of books entitled *Seimei no jisso* (Truth of Life) published by *Seicho no ie* (literally, The House of Growing Life), a religious movement which had become popular in Japan only a decade before Kitagawa had been incarcerated. The religious movement, led by Masaharu Taniguchi (1893-1985) attracted Japanese both in Japan and overseas during the dark period of Japan's war years (1931-1945). The movement emphasized optimism, moral positivism, patriotism, and emperor worship. It claims that it is not a religion but a moral and philosophical way of thinking and living which transcends and embraces all other religions.

The reader of the Kitagawa letters will see how he tried to apply the *Seicho no ie* teaching to his everyday life while in confinement and how he regarded his experience as a god-given opportunity to train and better himself to reach a higher moral existence. His religious redirection is an interesting contrast with the attitude of Koichiro Miyazaki who was living in the same camp and who apparently did not resort to any particular religion.

L E T T E R S

June 28, 1942

On the 16th, 9:18 p.m., the special train loaded with 190 of our comrades left Vancouver. We passed through several tunnels and at dusk of the 17th we reached the border of the province of Alberta where the marker stands which says, "5,332 feet above sea level." After we passed Lake Louise, we began to see herds of deer and several groups (families) of three or four moose, which remained calm almost as if they did not notice the train. This view reminded me of a peaceful park, like the Pacific Ocean without waves. The train continued for 200 miles of prairie and passed Shreiber . . . afternoon of the 19th. We went on for two more hours before we finally arrived in this camp. I wanted to send a telegram to you immediately but we were not allowed to. I am sorry. But I hope each family was informed of our arrival by the authorities.

This camp is pretty well-equipped and from our group professionals were selected to become kitchen workers. So although the quantity is small, the food is quite tasty. The bugle wakes us at 6:30 in the morning. Breakfast is at 7:00, lunch at 12:00, and supper at 5:30. There are two roll calls: at 8:00 in the morning and at 9:30 in the evening. When we arrived here, they were still heating with the wood stove day and night. But two or three days ago, we stopped heating in the daytime. In this region, the air is so dry that it is said to be very good for pneumonia and rheumatic problems. My upper right arm which was always aching is fine now, so I regard this new situation almost as if it were a spa. We all started to do some work for exercise. It was decided that I would begin working as a tailor, along with Mr. Kawai and Mr. Kimura, but since we still don't have a sewing machine, we can't begin to work. So please send me a thimble along with number 4 and 16 needles.

Please do not force yourself to work too hard, and take care. Please send my regards to the people from Duncan.

July 5, 1942

Already one month has passed since I had to leave you and it will probably be two months before this letter reaches you. How have you been? As

Morning roll call at Angler prison camp.

Courtesy of Kotoma Kitagawa

I read my last year's diary, I worry that your health might be as poor as it was then. I write just to get a response from my letter. It takes such a long time, so my worry just accumulates. But what can a prisoner like myself do? The only hope is to take care of oneself and stay healthy. Please do not over-exert yourself. Thank God I am fine. It is hard to get up so early for someone like myself who likes to sleep late, but this regular disciplined life must be very good for the health. When I am off duty, I walk round and round inside the fence, so they gave me the nickname of "Bear in the Zoo." I wish to do some calligraphy exercises but I can't because there is no paper. But I still can train my body and mind. As yet we have had no newspapers or any news from outside. I have no idea what is happening in Vancouver and other places. Please send me some news but only within the limits of this country's laws. I only wish we could read newspapers but negotiations are underway and I wonder how the people from Duncan are doing in Hastings Park. Even though I can't do anything, I still can't help worrying about those in frail health. Please send my best regards . . .

August 2, 1942

I received your letter yesterday. Thank you for the photograph. You say you gained five pounds. Nothing can make me happier than this news. You say that Chinese people are now living in our house in Duncan. It does not matter who is living there. I hope that the government will settle the problem once peaceful times return. They say people in the interior camps like Slocan are living in tents. Even where you have been living now, a tent would be too cold for you with delicate health, and I doubt very much that you could survive winter there. Please do not listen to rumours. Don't follow what other people do, and instead please listen to your own better judgement.

August 8, 1942

We have almost reached the middle of August. I don't find it too hot. On the fourth we had a heavy frost but in the last two or three days it has become quite hot again. If it doesn't get hotter than now, for a person like myself who is not crazy about heat, this is a pleasant place. It's as if we were staying in a resort to escape the hot weather. However, the idea of winter overwhelms me. I hear the temperature will go down to 40 or 50 below zero. They say it was a pretty warm winter last year, but still the temperature went down to minus 40. I try to train myself in order to be able to bear the severe cold . . . I also feel sunbathing helps. When I have time I read books and try to discipline my mind as well.

The other day I was called out by the Custodian [of Alien Property] and was told that our house had been rented for $35. They showed me a statement with a list of things that we left behind in the house, but I noted that the items listed are only ten percent of what we actually left. As far as I am concerned, I don't want to rent the house and store out to somebody else, but if I really have to, I want them to record all we have in our house and store [with a responsible witness] and then rent it out. What the Custodian has done so far does not please me because they did not check with us before they rented our house. At the time of the evacuation, although we tried to call them many times, they refused to come and see us.

August 17, 1942

. . . We are living an easy and uneventful life, but there are so many rumours going around about the evacuation and these stir up our minds. Our families in Vancouver send us all kinds of presents, but there are many things that cannot be received here. You do not have to send anything, since your good intentions might be in vain. But for the young men here, if you could send them pictures of young girls, they would be thrilled. Health first! Regards to people from Duncan.

August 23, 1942

A major event struck us suddenly last night. They said those who wish to go to Japan under the POW exchange program could apply immediately. But how can you decide such a thing on the spur of the moment? I had to think all night last night and came to the conclusion that I will apply. I already have. So, from now on, I want you to be ready to return to Japan at any time, in case I am accepted. Some information might reach you too, but we would not be able to take too many things with us. Even if we had to depart from different places, we will probably end up on the same boat, do not worry about that. T., W., and Y. have also applied. I am still trying to do something about the things we left in Duncan, but even if things do not go as we wish, please give them up as if we had been hit by earthquake.

September 21, 1942

I received your card dated September 2nd on the 16th. I was shocked to hear that Mr. Yoneda passed away. I can imagine the sadness and bereavement that Mrs. Yoneda and others must be feeling. You tell me that he died after surgery and I wonder what kind of illness he was suffering from. I remember that he had a gallstone condition, so I wonder if this is related to that. Anyway, I feel sorry. It's unfortunate that he should die at a time like this, when even a good funeral cannot be held.

. . .

As to preparations for our trip back to Japan, please get as much information as possible and be ready. Even if you have bought things and packed our belongings, they might not allow you to take them. Since censorship is severe these days, I don't want to write anything against regulations and have it burned, and so I cannot write freely. Moreover, I don't receive your letters these days and so I don't have much to say. Therefore I will stop here . . .

October 4, 1942

. . . According to rumours, all the Japanese remaining in Hastings Park were removed by the end of September. I'm worried. Now I don't know where to send my letters to you. I thought that I should wait until I received your letter but I don't know when that will be. I cannot just wait like this.

Wherever you are, if only you are healthy, nothing can make me happier. After all, this is wartime. We know that we have to be patient about the lack of freedom in our lives. Recently we received a lot of Japanese magazines, which I can borrow and read. There are many books on Personal Development so I am taking advantage of this opportunity and am reading to train myself. As for returning to Japan, I have stopped brooding over it. If we go back, that's fine, but if we stay here, that's fine too. The longer I stay here, the longer time I will have for self-improvement. The more restricted my life is now, the more I will appreciate my freedom later. The only thing I worry about is your health. I am very health conscious. As I wrote to you last month, in the morning I rub myself with a cold towel and practice abdominal breathing for one hour. Except in rainy weather, I make sure that I walk, and also I am very careful about eating. I read before and after meals. the roll calls are now at 7:25, earlier than before. But Lights Out is still 10:30. As a result, we have more time for reading and it is very good for our spiritual training. I am very grateful. The young boys from Duncan are always studying and showing a lot of promise.

October 18, 1942

As the leaves started changing colour, a violent wind blew them away and now we see only naked trees standing sadly. I remember with nostalgia those days when we went into the mountains to look for *matsutake* mushrooms . . . [From somebody else's mail] I learned that you people were moving to Slocan around the 26th [of September]. I still haven't received your letter and do not know what has been happening. I just imagine the hardship that you have been going through.

. . .

November 24, 1942

Yesterday I received your fifth letter dated November 4th from Slocan. I am glad to hear that you are well, despite the snow and the cold weather. If you were sickly as in the old days, how could I stay calm? I can only thank God for his protection.

Since the 16th, I've been on night shift. Three stoves and the boiler for the bath and bathroom stove, for a total of five stoves. An older person is in charge until ten o'clock and then I get up to take over until morning. I have plenty of time to read, and recently have time to practice calligraphy, copying texts from No theatre for other people. I am very glad to do it because it's good for me. Yesterday was Sunday and supper was chicken rice. For the first time in six or seven months I could taste the chicken. Since one chicken has to be shared by about twelve people, they cannot roast or fry it but instead they made it into curried rice and it was a success. What can you do with sixty or so chickens for so many of us? We have only one month and a bit before Christmas. At Christmas time we might be able to see chicken in our dish one more time.

November 29, 1942

I too am well but if you ask me if I'm lonely I have to say yes. But thanks to my self-training I can feel that any hardship is a pleasure. I am looking forward to a new life with you. By going through this difficult time, your health will be strengthened and you will regain your weight and happy temperament. Recently I have been reading books from *Seicho no ie* and have come to realize how much my imperfection caused suffering in you. The mental pain that I caused was so great that you became ill. Because of your illness, I too suffered quite a bit but in my case it was deserved. Now for the first time I regret from the bottom of my heart and feel sorry for you. Although in the past I felt that I came to enlightenment, I now know that it was not real. I knew that I was in the wrong, but I didn't realize that it caused your illness. I came to this realization by reading the text over and over again. Please be happy for me for coming to this state of mind. I just cannot help being grateful to God for putting me in this situation. We did lose our life entirely, but we now have gained more than that. I ask you to read the books from *Seicho no ie*.

[Letter to Miss O.]

December 5, 1942

"Blessed are they that mourn, for they shall be consoled."

As this saying implies, we are the fortunate ones. We are fortunate enough to encounter such difficult circumstances. We may make better use of these hardships and improve ourselves. In the past, Japanese workers overseas were automatically associated with money-making, but this war is going to be a turning-point and we immigrants must realize that we are here not to make money but for our glorious mission to spread the great Japanese imperial ways. Each person represents Japan and is a pioneer of our nation. We must swear to embody the Japanese way of loyalty and filial respect and become examples for people. In order to realize the great ideal, one must set aside his own profit and discard petty thoughts, and act as a representative of his nation. For the great cause, small causes should be set aside. Let us restrain ourselves in order to advance on the great path. Fortunately, there is a library here and a high school and I am studying hard to improve myself. The young men from the Duncan district are all well and studying hard to prepare for the future. So please remain assured and live in harmony with your companions.

[*Letters to his wife*]

January 2, 1943

Happy New Year. Thank you for your help in the year to come.

The year of great changes has passed like a dream and another glorious year begun with two bottles of beer for each person. I feel a little tipsy. We had a Japanese meal with turkey and two or three drops of soy sauce. It is impossible to describe how tasty it was. How lucky we are to have Happy New Year like this. This is going to be the first year of my new life after being reborn as a painless child of God. And I hope that you too will live this year as a divine child free of suffering. If you can detach from yourself, life won't be so hard. Suffering and illness are caused by selfishness. So let us move ahead without self. This year of the Sheep will be a good year for us.

The day before Christmas I received your chocolate. These days, chocolate is very rare and hard to get . . . Thank you. The people from New Denver sent us cigarettes. We also received cakes and Christmas cards from Greenwood. A letter from Slocan told us that they sent us something but we haven't received it yet.

January 11, 1943

On the fifth we received a telegram stating that the Foreign Minister of the Great Japanese Empire on New Year's Eve had kindly given a message of congratulations at the start of yet another glorious year, to all the Japanese prisoners of war. All of us are moved.

On the seventh I was called out by the Custodians. They asked me where my war savings are, so I informed them that you have them. When they come to contact you, just let them handle the matter. I also told them that the insurance contract is in the bank. They will take care of it. We can only let God watch over us. Anyway, take good care of yourself and best regards to everyone. I received your ninth and tenth letters today, January 10th, on the anniversary of my father's death.

February 8, 1943

Your letter dated January 16th was received on the 6th of February. I'm glad to hear that you are well despite the very cold weather. I am also well and day by day I feel myself becoming younger. In this camp I finally met someone who is also a reader of *Seimei no jisso*, text books of

Japanese Canadian internees being released
from POW Camp in Angler, Ontario, 1946.

Courtesy of Japanese Canadian Cultural Centre.

the *Seicho no ie*. I borrowed the other volumes and enjoy reading daily. The time is now going so fast that I sometimes want to slow it down. I am grateful that my mental state changes as I read. It is said that by reading these books even far- and near-sightedness can be corrected. But I guess I haven't reached that level because I still need glasses. It is true that I am now able to read tiny characters for four or five hours straight without getting tired. I am proud of this achievement. By the time I see you again, I hope to read books without glasses.

. . .

[As to property that we left behind], even though we are enemy aliens, they are not allowed to do inhuman things to us. Suddenly I began to worry about our cat Miko left behind in Duncan. I gave ten dollars to the Custodian to give to the shoe repair store next door, so that they could buy milk. I wanted to consult with you, but as I was quite concerned, I went ahead and did it.

Only good things have been happening today. I dreamt of my late sister whom I had never met.

February 20, 1943

I am glad to receive your letter and know that you are doing well, and have recently been reading *Seimei no jisso*. I no longer have to worry about you.

[Letter to Miss O.]

March 1, 1943

I received your letter on the 27th. What a lucky day it was! I received four letters including yours. Imagine the scene as I open letters like a child opening Christmas presents.

I did some research on boldness and I came to the conclusion that there is no hope for my boldness, so I decided to shave my head. If you could see me now, I'm sure your life would be lengthened by a year or two. Your mama would laugh until she cried. I wish I could go home to make everyone laugh. But no, I'm a *Kyushu*[2] boy, and even if my life was threatened I would never do such a cowardly thing. There are some young people at the camp who wish to leave, without the strong will to resist the temptation of joining in happiness with others. Fortunately, your big brother refused to go along with them. He is determined to obey his mama's wish. So I suggest that your mama write to him directly. Under the present circumstances, we should not be selfish . . . We must understand our situation and we have to be very clear about our direction. We are enemy aliens. So how can we volunteer to work for our enemies' industry? It's another story if we are forced to do so. I am sorry I sound dark and serious.

[Letter to Mrs. T.]

April 11, 1943

Just as the seasons change from summer to fall, fall to winter, people's minds also change. When we all came to this place, our minds were like fresh snow. But like spring snow, the minds of some of our campmates are now beginning to melt, and they now begin to float like butterflies in search of spring flowers. There are rumours that they will be leaving this camp soon, but I am happy that our Duncan group, with only a few exceptions, remains strong. So please tell my friends not to worry. I am convinced that peaceful days will come to us soon. Day by day, I look forward to that time.

[Letters to his wife]

May 2, 1943

It's getting warmer and the snow has mostly disappeared. We now have roll calls outdoors. It feels good. On the 29th of April [the Emperor's birthday was celebrated], after the ceremony, we had a variety show. Everyone gathered together and it became a very cheerful event. I was impressed by how much talent we have among us.

The *New Canadian*[3] of April 10 reports that there will be a hearing on the issue of confiscated property and they are urging readers to support it by giving donations. It is ridiculous to try to question what has been decided in the name of the War Measures Act. So even if they knock on your door for a contribution, I don't think we should even consider it. Our property has already been put into the hands of God. I believe that

生長の家九州別格本山第35回練成会

During the war years Kensuke Kitagawa became a follower of Seicho no ie, a religious movement which had become popular in Japan only a decade before Kitagawa had been incarcerated. In the 1960s, Mr. & Mrs. Kitagawa attended a Seicho no ie training camp in Kyushu, Japan. (In dark clothing, seated in second row).

we should trust God just as we trust our parents.

On April 27, Doctor Hori left the camp. I guess he will go to your area to pick up his parents and then move to a Japanese settlement in Eastern Canada. On the 29th, a young boy who has been very sick since summer was transferred to New Denver hospital. There does not seem to be much hope. I am sorry. With his departure there isn't any seriously sick person remaining here. But the release of Doctor Hori makes the people here uneasy. As for me, I have no fear. Every day is a precious day for self-training, so the longer I have to stay here, the better I grow.

May 9, 1943

On the third, a person in charge of the mail let me know that a parcel had arrived for me so I thought it was a pen I had asked you to send me. I hurried off and was surprised to find a big box. I tried to guess what it was, but could not. I opened it as if I was Taro [opening the box he brought back from Dragon Castle at the sea bottom].[4] Then I found a very fine [artificial] wisteria bough covered with flowers. In this desolate camp landscape it's a precious gift, not only for myself, but for many people. It's so realistic that someone has said he cannot help leaning close to smell it. But I said, "At least it smells like my wife!" They all laughed hard and said they were jealous. I'm very glad that everybody is happy with it . . . Two or three other gifts came for others, but as I expected yours was the best one.

May 15, 1943

. . .

I have been looking at the wisteria bough every day. But I feel bad about monopolizing it for myself, so I hung it higher up on the wall so that everybody can see. Thank you.

May 21, 1943

. . .

Even in this land of severe cold, warm weather is gaining ground and life has become easier. I continue to be very healthy. Since the 18th I have been working outside from 8:30 to around 4:00 with W. and others. I never feel any fatigue. As a certain book says, there are three commandments for long life: (1) Do not get angry. You never feel good after getting upset. Anger always accompanies suffering. (2) Keep your stomach only 80% full. Refrain from luxurious food and excessive eating. (3) Respect all forms of life and treat them well.

May 28, 1943

I still look at the wisteria branch that you sent me which is on the wall. As I slept in the lower bunk, a haiku came to me:

Wisteria flowers:
But double-decker bed
Is in my way

I wonder how you interpret this poem. Guess where my mind is?

N O T E S

1. Ken Adachi, *The Enemy That Never Was* (Toronto: McClelland and Stewart, 1976) 340.

2. In Japan, men from the southern island of Kyushu tend to see themselves as tough and strong-minded.

3. *The New Canadian* was the first newspaper for Japanese Canadians published by the Nisei, and it was the only newspaper allowed to continue publishing during the war.

Slocan
Diary

Kaoru Ikeda

Slocan Diary

KAORU IKEDA

Editor's Introduction

I met Mrs. Chisato Tokunaga for the first time at the "Senior Drop In" which takes place every week at Montreal's Japanese Canadian Cultural Centre. I was excited to meet the woman who was the daughter of Arichika Ikeda, one of the pioneers of Japanese Canadian history. Through her I thought I might be able to discover, and get a better feeling for, those early pioneer days. In fact, what she told me that first day, was not about Japanese-Canadian history but rather the terrible reality of apartheid and racism in South Africa. I learned later that one of her daughters is married to a black Anglican bishop in Trinidad and was committed to the advancement of oppressed blacks.

I visited Mrs. Tokunaga in her small apartment in Montreal several times. She showed me many volumes of photo albums, books her father had published in Japan some ninety years ago, his notebooks, and her mother's diaries. I was most interested in the "Slocan Diary" that her mother, Kaoru Ikeda, kept during the war years while in the "relocation" camp at Slocan, British Columbia.

Kaoru Ikeda, was born in 1875 in Niigata Prefecture. After marrying Arichika Ikeda from the same prefecture, she came to Canada in 1914. She spent the rest of her life in Canada. Arichika Ikeda (1864-1939) is known as one of the Japanese pioneers of North America. He arrived in the United States in 1890, and was part of the colonization of northern

California. He joined the Klondike Gold Rush in the Yukon, spent time in Alaska and later moved to British Columbia and began mining minerals. Today there is a bay on the British Columbia coast which bears his name.

After her husband died in Vancouver in 1939, Kaoru Ikeda, who was already a naturalized Canadian, remained in Canada with her children and grandchildren. When Japan attacked Pearl Harbour in December 1941 she was sixty-six years old. In June of the following year Kaoru Ikeda was forced to abandon her house and move with the family of her daughter, Chisato, to the interior of British Columbia. She spent three years at the Slocan "relocation camp" and then another year in the New Denver, British Columbia camp. While waiting to resettle elsewhere she became sick and died in the spring of 1946, less than a year after World War II ended.

The Slocan Diary are excerpts from a journal that Kaoru Ikeda wrote over a two-year period starting in December 1942 and ending in December 1944. The first third of her 120-page diary is in fact a memoir written in December 1942 looking back at the past year. This part was probably written on the basis of notes that she had accumulated over the year. The remaining two-thirds of her diary are about daily life in the "relocation camps." In the second year of her diary, traditional Japanese poems called *haiku* and *tanka* began to play a more important role. Her diary portrays a life of cooking, gathering food, being surrounded by nature, and family health. These daily routines are accentuated by the occasional festival and rites of passage. We are shown a way of collective living where friends and family members, young and old, gather to exchange their knowledge, console one another, and put their feelings into traditional Japanese poetic forms.

However, in this record of the apparently peaceful life in the interior camps, the shadow of war does make itself felt. The diary tells us of conflicts among different Japanese-Canadian factions, the bureaucracy and betrayal of the Canadian government, and the state of the war in which Japan was increasingly in crisis. Despite the author's anger towards the Canadian government, her sympathy for the Nisei generation that insisted on their Canadian citizenship, grew. On the one hand she accepts her fate as an enemy alien with resignation, while on the other, she quietly wishes a better future for the younger generations and their recovery after the war. At the end of 1943 she wrote this *tanka* poem:

I thought
It would only be temporary
In this Mountain country
Accumulate another year
As snow deepens

The following year, 1944, her health deteriorated. On her birthday in November, she wrote: "I was afraid that I would not be able to live until this birthday but I am grateful to have made it." The last entry of the diary is December 7, which is the third anniversary of Pearl Harbour. The last two sentences describe her thoughts about the War:

. . . The difference between reality and propaganda is now hard to distinguish. I cannot believe everything that is reported. Because we cannot hear the news from Japan we are in a constant state of anxiety.

After Pearl Harbour

Oh, 7th of December! What bewildering and confusing days we have been living since Pearl Harbour. With the great mission to establish world peace, Japan is fighting with great success to the amazement of the world. As Japanese we feel proud of our country and pray that our advances continue until our final victory.

The year before last, after Canada joined the war in support of England, we Japanese in Canada contributed all the resources we had: buying Victory Bonds, making donations for national defence and the Red Cross. Even our children at school saved their pocket money to buy saving stamps, while housewives found the time, despite already busy days, to sew and knit for the Red Cross. We did all we could to prove that we were loyal Canadian citizens. How did the authorities respond to our efforts? They carried their vigilance to extremes: confiscating all firearms owned by Japanese Canadians, forbidding the use of gunpowder even for industrial purposes, drawing up a registry of our names, and taking our fingerprints. They began to treat us with increasing severity. Once Japan joined the war against America and Britain, executive members of firms which had direct ties with Japan were arrested and jailed. The number of arrests increased and later, I heard, there were many arrests among those who refused to go into the camps.

On the sea, all the Nikkei fishermen had to hand over their boats to the government; while on land, car, camera, and radio ownership or operation were forbidden and confiscated from us. Beginning on the night of the 7th, both in the United States and Canada, blackouts were in effect in the Pacific Coast area and the night became pitch black. Although this did not last more than a few days, it was enough to create rumours and fear among the population that Japan was coming to bomb them and that the Japanese would organize riots. Mobs harassed the Japanese and I even heard they set fire to homes and they beat people up wherever they could find them.

The federal government has been at a loss, not knowing exactly how to deal with us Japanese in Canada. Orders keep changing without any guiding principle. The recklessness and confusion that they displayed while confiscating our fishing boats demonstrated especially well how shocked they were by the first air attacks and how they feared the Japanese. Was this the behaviour of a great country? There have been many stories of this kind, silly enough even to make an old woman like me burst into laughter.

According to Prime Minister King's original announcement from Ottawa, only those with Japanese citizenship would be removed from British Columbia and Nisei born in Canada and naturalized Canadians would be allowed to stay where they were. However, the faction of British Columbia politicians led by Halford Wilson, with their anti-Japanese platform, persistently urged the government to revoke our business licenses, take away our lands and property, and imprison us as enemy aliens. These attitudes incited the public against us and success-fully shaped Ottawa's policies. As a result, Ottawa gave the British Columbia Security Commission full powers to have all Nikkei displaced a minimum of a 100 miles inland from any coast. The foundation of our community created by more than half a century of our pioneers' sweat and blood was destroyed. The lands, property and businesses that we, 22,000 compatriots, had achieved with many years of hard work, were taken from us and we were herded to the interior of the province.

The Days Before Removal

Our men who had been working in factories, lumber camps and other places were all dismissed and exiled from Vancouver. They were sent to work in road camps in Ontario, Alberta and the in the interior of British Columbia. They were separated from women, children and older people unable to work, who would be placed in barracks in Hastings Park. Since those who live in Vancouver were also being gradually sent away to road camps there was so much confusion in the Powell Street area that you would have thought it was the scene of a fire. At the beginning of March, K.-san was sent to a place called Hope. A curfew was imposed from March 2nd, forbidding any Japanese to be outside between seven in the evening and seven at morning. Against these and other pressures we have not a single weapon to defend ourselves. As enemy aliens we could not claim the protection of the law and even if we were kicked around we could do nothing but grit our teeth, swallow our tears, and obey orders.

In the middle of this turmoil, Mr. K.T., who had been sick since the year before, passed away. I heard that, unfortunately, a sudden decline in the state of his health came in the middle of the night. A doctor was phoned but the police would not permit a visit nor would they allow anyone to run over and fetch Mrs. H., Mr. K.T.'s sister who lived one block over. By dawn he was dead. The thing his wife found the most regrettable was that he could not receive a doctor's care up to the end.

My son-in-law Tokunaga, even after taking ill last year, took on all the administrative responsibilities for a lumber company, which allowed him little time for rest; even when he got sick with the flu he could not take time off. On top of this the tension he felt when negotiating with hostile whites and the worry of having our future livelihood snatched away, had tired him body and soul. Chisato was gravely concerned as Tokunaga became painfully haggard and drawn.

My son Arimoto who had left Ocean Falls and had joined us in Vancouver was living with us as he had not been told to report to Hastings Park. But he was finally sent away to a road camp, a place called Taft, on April 13th. Chisato and the rest of us were greatly worried that Tokunaga would also be sent to a camp but fortunately the doctor's diagnosis was that while he was not sick, he was definitely not eligible to work. To my tremendous relief he was given permission to relocate with the rest of our family. Wealthier people were given certain choices as to where they could live on their own resources. They were allowed to take all of their household goods with them, but the burden was a heavy one because they had to pay all moving and living costs themselves, naturally most people cannot afford it.

Each of the church denominations was co-operating with the Security Commission on behalf of its followers, to rent a plot of land where they could be moved to. It seemed natural for the Japanese pastors who worked hard for their compatriots and followers, but I could not help feeling grateful and happy to the point of shedding tears to see *hakujin* missionaries work devotedly to help the Japanese. The necessary arrangements for places to live and fuel were to be handled by the Commission. The only thing we would have to pay ourselves would be the cost of food. This way the expense would be quite low. My family were not really members of a church but when we heard that non-members could go with them we applied to the Anglican church.

Catholics were going to Greenwood, Anglicans to Slocan, the United Church people to Kaslo and the Buddhists to Sandon. All could have been described as "ghost towns." Decades earlier they had been prosperous mining towns, but the mines had been abandoned and the buildings, large and small, were decrepit and deserted. They were to be renovated under the auspices of the Commission and turned into homes. I couldn't imagine what sort of places they were. In May we were finally leaving for these camps.

An agent took charge of the house and all our business matters were to be entrusted to him. We were told that the house rent was to be kept by the government and we were not to receive it. We sold off most of the furniture but since the buyer took advantage of our situation we got very little for it. I was mortified, but there was no point in complaining when almost every Japanese was in the same position. All our possessions, house, land, and store, were listed and handed over to the government Custodian. All we could do was to gnash our teeth, hold back our tears, and head for the interior.

Departure

On Wednesday, June 3rd, one hundred and forty people, including us, were assembled and sent to Slocan, British Columbia. Two trains had gone at the end of May and this was the third one.

The day before departure I cut as many flowers from the garden as I could and went to visit the family graves. I offered the flowers to my dead husband, my son Ken, and my older brother, and bid farewell to them all. Not knowing when I would be able to come back to visit their graves, I could not help but weep. When my husband passed away, although I knew he had a full life, my sadness was profound. However, now that we faced these recent disturbances, I began to feel that his death was timely. With his various connections to Japan, if he had been alive, he would have been put in jail. Even so it was much better to have died before being exiled to a godforsaken "ghost town" and forced into a miserable life in his old age. He was a happy man to die surrounded by his family and friends.

We took rice to the T.'s house, cooked it and made many rice balls to stuff in our lunch boxes. We also packed our bags with bread, butter, roast chicken, canned goods, and fruits to take with us on the long trip. This was enough food for about three or four days. Soon my daughter's family came to join us for a farewell dinner that Mr. and Mrs. T. kindly prepared for us. They made *mame* and rice and wished us good health.[1] Although Mrs. T.'s homecooking was always delicious, that day the miso soup and the boiled food was especially tasty. As the excellence of the food touched me, I wondered if the day would come when we could again share a meal. My heart was heavy.

We said goodbye, got into the car and left for the CPR station arriving at six o'clock. Friends and acquaintances were there to see us off. The platform was noisy and crowded with so many people saying goodbye. At six-thirty we boarded the train. The Mounted Police examined each of us and checked our names off against a registry. Every passenger was handed a dollar to pay for a meal on the train. I again tried hard to control my tears and be silent while experiencing such humiliation. I kept repeating to myself, "We are no longer Canadian citizens, we are Japanese taken prisoner in an enemy country; behind us stands the national dignity of great Japan. One day we will again have our dignity. One day . . ."

At seven o'clock the train slowly pulled out. I felt hollow as I was being driven away from the place where I had lived for nearly thirty years. At rail crossings here and there, crowds of Japanese gathered to wave and call out their good wishes. On a bluff near the outskirts of town the T. family were sadly waving goodbye. All of us were moved to wave handkerchiefs out the windows, until we were lost from view.

Exiled at Slocan

Surrounded by dark green hills and a mirror-like lake, Slocan presents some fine scenery. It's just like a summer resort and the water is so clean that it runs through pipes which go directly into the kitchens. We must think it lucky to move to a place like this, since there are said to be camps where water is not in such abundant supply.

The greater part of the Slocan Valley spreads out widely around the clear stream which flows from Lake Slocan. This area was to be the home of the Japanese evacuees. When I arrived there were about five hundred of us, but I heard that there were plans to bring in four to five thousand people. There were about three hundred or so *hakujin* settlers already living in the area. Officials at the Commission office were kind enough

Until shacks could be built many evacuees
in the Slocan Valley had to live in tents.

Courtesy of Kotoma Kitagawa

but what gave us an unexpected pleasure were the smiles and friendliness of the local *hakujin*. It relieved my fears somewhat and I began to think that living in exile would not be as bad as we thought it would be.

We stayed in a big hall on the outskirts of town for exactly one week, until Tokunaga and the others had the luck to find an empty house. After getting the approval of Hartley, the Commission director, we moved into our house. Other people also settled into various buildings, rooms and empty houses which they renovated. Friday the 12th of June, was clear and sunny, for many days before it rained, but luckily it cleared up for our move.

A mile or so into the mountains, to the South East of the town of Slocan there was what remained of a silver mine. There were a number of abandoned buildings, large and small, but since no more than five or six years had gone by since they were used they still looked new. The main building was large enough to be divided into apartments and over twenty Japanese were working hard as carpenters to make the building suitable for the evacuees to occupy. The small building which was at the foot of the hill was assigned to us. It was the former mine office. Its light brown paint was still in good condition and it had many large windows which let in a lot of light.

The five people in our family were given one house for us to live in together. This was a fortunate exception, which caused envy and jealousy among other Japanese.[2]

Here we are surrounded by hills and it is not very convenient to run errands and shop in town but the peace and quiet is worth the trouble. From the back of the house a sloping path rises to the top of the hill. On one side of the path there is a high cliff on top of which sits a gloomy forest. There seems to be good pasture in the mountains, because morning and evening there are boys leading herds of cattle along the trail, bells around their necks ringing *karan, karan*. When we see something like that, we know we've arrived in the country! Watching these cows is one of our pleasures, giving us a mellow feeling, somehow. We have asked the herdsmen to deliver us a bottle of fresh milk everyday.

Caught up in play
Left behind by the herd
Surprised young calves
Run to catch up —
How lovely!

Looking back
As their children straggle
In wayside grass —
Cow mothers mooing
Sorrowfully

Tokunaga acquired some scrap lumber from the nearby mill and made shelves. The rest of us were also busy putting plates, food and other small things in order. We began to clear the land around the house and made a garden. We planted lettuce, radishes and beans although it was a bit late in the season. We also transplanted chrysanthemums, trefoil, and coltsfoot that we had uprooted in such a hurry the morning we left Vancouver. There were so many tough thickets, dead trees and a network of bracken roots that a spade wouldn't even break through, so that even with Chisato and the kids helping, it was dreadful back-breaking labour for Tokunaga.

The 21st was the anniversary of Ikeda's death, but we could not visit him at his grave. His photograph, enlarged and framed, was hung on the kitchen wall. Since there were plenty of little lilies blooming behind our house, I picked some, put them in a small empty bottle and left them as an offering on the makeshift altar that Tokunaga had nailed together from a piece of board. I consulted with Chisato about some favourite dish of her father's we could offer him, but what could we get our hands on in such a remote place? With some leftover flour and red bean paste we made dumplings and boiled some fiddleheads we picked on the mountain. We put these dishes in front of a framed photograph of Ikeda as an offering and we humbly shared a meal with him. I am sure my deceased husband must have been surprised to have this service in such unfamiliar, poor surroundings. It made me think of how he loved fiddleheads. Every year we went to the woods near Burnaby to pick them.

Bored with inactivity, Tokunaga asked Mr. Hartley at the Commission to give him some work. He thought work would be better for his health. It so happened that they needed somebody in the accounts department and he was able to start right away. In order not to create unemployment problems the Commission tried to supply work to as many Japanese as possible. Carpenters and skilled craftsmen, people to collect firewood from the forests, others to transport and chop it, warehouse hands, truck drivers, janitors, bath house workers, stovepipe cleaners, sales people in shops, hospital attendants, busboys and waitresses in restaurants. There were over a thousand people in all. Tokunaga became very busy, pressured by his responsibilities which made me worry for his health.

Wages were as small as they were in the road camps but since we did not have to pay for housing we made enough to buy food. The old and the sick who could not work or did not receive any money from family members working in road camps were given government assistance. There were many people with complaints, but considering that we were regarded as enemy aliens I thought we should be rather thankful for the generous way the authorities in Slocan were treating us.

The Role of the Old

In mid-October, Tokunaga's long time friend Mr. M. and his family arrived. Sadly, Mr. M. looked drawn and weak after suffering from a long illness. The chrysanthemums that we had planted in our garden were fortunately budding and were beginning to bloom golden flowers, so I gave him a bunch as an expression of sympathy. He looked very happy and surprised to see chrysanthemums in such a remote place.

Fortunately I was extremely healthy, I had completely recovered from the hay fever from which I suffered so much in Vancouver. In my old age I was unable to be much use in the household and felt sorry for my daughter and her husband to have a burden like me on their shoulders. If I fell sick or died in such an inconvenient place not only would I feel miserable but it would be a great inconvenience for my family and friends. With this in mind I swore to myself that I would never put myself in that position and I prayed that I could maintain my health until peace time would come again. Also I prayed that my whole family would be kept safe.

Since I never much liked the hustle and bustle of the city, I would just as gladly be living on the slopes of a mountain where we could hike out back daily. We found huckleberry bushes everywhere in the woods. In August when the berries became dark red and ripe, we picked and ate them with sugar and milk — they were so delicious. After having heard that the local people gathered bushels of them to make jam, we too went to pick and make jam two or three times. Both the colour and the taste were first class. Everyday, however warm it was, I put on a sweater and two pairs of socks as protection against the mosquitos, and wandered off into the mountains. Chisato would see me off, making fun of my outfit and wishing me luck on my quest.

Sometimes I was frightened to find big paw prints and bear droppings in the mountains, but my forays were too much fun for me to stop. I could only hope that they wouldn't come out during the day. I had also heard that noise would scare them off, so I loudly sang made-up songs as I walked. If somebody had seen me they would have thought I was crazy. At this thought I burst into laughter.

Picking berries
I happened on a bearprint
In the Slocan mountains

The fall scenery of Slocan was especially fine. From the mountain tops we could see the clear water of the lakes down below. The mixed yellows of the willows and deciduous trees against the deep green of the mountains and the red maples composed a beautiful canvas. When the berry season had passed we began to gather pine cones and dead twigs. Some of the cones were extraordinarily large, ranging from five to eight sun.[3] And they were filled with so much sap, they burned extremely well in our morning fire.

Mountain life
Gathering fallen wood
The right job for an old one

Searching for mushrooms was also fun. The mountains being so full of pine, one would expect matsutake mushrooms to appear.[4] So on Sundays there were many people who went hiking in search of matsutake mushrooms but could not find any. Anyway, whatever place one lives in offers unique pleasures.

Waking on the morning of October 31st, we were all amazed to discover a blanket of pure white snow. Although previous mornings had been cold and frosty, no one could have imagined that we would have snow so soon. Looking at each other, somebody said what we were all thinking: "We should have known better, Slocan is not Vancouver!" That night was Halloween but how could it mean anything in this place. Mariko discovered a few fireworks that were left over from the year before. After dark we divided some apples and fireworks with the children across the way until they had two or three each. Then to everyone's delight we set off a firework display.

Being Japanese

At long last the turmoil of the evacuation has settled down a little. They say around 5,000 Japanese are in the Slocan area. Lemon Creek, which is seven miles from town, has 1,800 people living there. Popoff, two miles away, has 1,200 and Bay Farm has 1,300. In the mining camp there are 80 people, including us. Since we are closest to Bay Farm we are included in their figure of 1,300. In the town of Slocan there are about 600 people.

Besides these, there is New Denver and Roseberry, both of which are twenty miles away. There is a bus that makes a round trip once a day. The Japanese there have formed an association called Hakko-kai[5] and the women have their own group. I hear that there are many brave women who don't hesitate to take their demands and grievances right to the Commission. They are quite ready to shout and pound the table until they are heard.

I hear a school is being built but because there is a lack of construction materials, the work goes very slowly. It may not be so bad for the little ones but for high school-aged kids it's not so simple. With nothing to do they won't learn anything good except to run loose and play around. Children whose parents keep a close eye on them will be all right, but there are, I hear, plenty of the other kind, whose the parents have money enough to be extravagant and have a good time gambling. Of course the young people will imitate them. Some, they say, will stake a bundle at gambling. There are also many ugly stories going around about the hoards of wild young kids who are out at movies and dance halls all night.

Even among the working men there are said to be those who slack off and fool around during working hours, saying that it's stupid to work seriously for such low wages. When I think how relentlessly we were driven into these circumstances it is understandable how some of us can lose heart and give up trying. But considering our position as displaced Japanese, shouldn't we try and keep a little more self-respect? Let's not despair over our fate. There will be a day when peace is restored to the world. Concerned people knit their brows in worry about what

In Slocan Mrs. Ikeda's daughter, Chisato, bought vegetables,
chickens and eggs from Doukhobors in their old-fashioned wagons.

Courtesy of Kotoma Kitagawa

is happening to our young people. When the time comes they will have to form a second wave of pioneers and make a new start for Japanese Canadian history.

The other night Tokunaga was talking with Mr. K. from across the way. They were saying that we have lost everything. We're back to where we started when we arrived in Canada — nothing to our names — and we'll have to begin our lives anew. Mr. K. was saying that although our freedom is restricted we are fairly secure, but real trouble will start when the war is over and we are released. He wondered how many of us would be ready for that day. If we let the younger generation continue on their present path, he raved, Japanese in Canada will end up beneath native Indians on the social scale.

Until now I have been a firm believer that Japanese are diligent, honest, humble, and kind. I have always been proud of my people. But since coming to this place I have heard so many stories that portray our people as capable of every kind of wickedness. Of course I realize it's only part of the truth. But still . . . it hurts me so much to hear that the Japanese people can be so base. Whatever our lot in life may become we must not despair; we must strive for a better future without ever losing our sense of gratitude.

Christmas in Slocan

Our neighbour Mrs. Urabe gave us two pretty boxes, one large and one small. They will serve as pickle casks. Several days ago when Chisato bought vegetables from the Doukhobors, (who come by in their old fashioned wagons to sell vegetables, chicken, eggs, etc.,) she said in passing to Mrs. Urabe, that she wished she had some barrels so that she could make pickles. Urabe-san kindly made her two casks for pickles. So we immediately bought cabbage. We are all happy to be able to make enough pickles to last us the whole winter. Chisato baked cookies and gave them to Urabe-san as thanks. It was also Urabe-san who was kind enough to bring the shovel he had made on the morning after another heavy snow fall. He is so kind.

The recent shortages of goods in this country are unbelievable. Last year aluminium products were disallowed, next it was rubber; gas rationing goes without saying. Similarly there are severe shortages of steel, and glass products are also restricted. So are shoes and other leather goods. Synthetics have replaced cotton and among foodstuffs, sugar was first rationed so there is hardly any candy available. We manage to buy a few sweets for Christmas, but jams and canned fruit are almost completely out of stock.

Time is passing so quickly, the year is almost over. There was a Christmas concert at the church and the children from Sunday school and kindergarten received some presents. Mariko was baptized on the Sunday of Christmas week. Despite a shortage of ingredients, Chisato managed to make a delicious Christmas cake and baked lots of cookies. We sent my son Arimoto cake and cookies as well as a leather half-coat. He was so pleased with his gifts that he sent, special delivery, a letter of thanks which arrived on Christmas Eve. I was most relieved to know that he was celebrating Christmas in good health.

Ayako and Mariko went into the mountains to find a small Christmas tree. Sadly their many Christmas ornaments were left in Vancouver, but they are imaginative enough to make their own. They waded through the snow and picked heaps of red berries they found thrusting up from the ground. Then they threaded them alternately with balls of cotton into 5- to 6-inch-long pieces and with these draped over the tree's branches, with some store-bought silver "icicles" sprinkled on, we had first class-decorations — quite lovely. Here and there we placed three or four birds I made from rags.

We had a wonderful dinner of delicious roast chicken which Chisato cooked in place of turkey, which our stove was too small to accommodate. Then a whole crowd of kids from the other building descended upon us to admire our Christmas tree. Each of them was very happy to receive the cookies and apples wrapped in paper and the little cloth birds and pin cushions that we divided among them. Later in the evening the older kids played cards exuberantly and were pleased when we served them Christmas cake and cocoa. Thus our Christmas turned out to be an unexpectedly merry time.

Later I heard a funny story about Christmas. The women's committee, which I mentioned before, made a resolution to demand turkey and Christmas presents for each family. Anybody could see that such demands would be rejected, but the most aggressive actually dared to go to the Commission with their demands. They were immediately refused. How brazen they could be! To make demands for things like electricity and water, which are necessities, is understandable and we can all see that the Commission has been trying hard to accommodate our needs within their limits. Now that we are given work and a wage, however small, I feel ashamed that people would demand to be given presents.

Now we are at the end of the year. In this wandering life of ours, there isn't much we can do to prepare for the New Year. Knowing that the children long for kuri-kinton I substituted peas for chestnuts and managed to make mame-kinton.[6] I chopped fruits into the left-over gelatin which made for a nice dessert. I cooked the few black beans that we had received from Mrs. M. and had been saving for this occasion. Chisato baked some cupcakes and made udon noodles which took her a long time. She cooked the chicken and made spaghetti, which was everyone's favourite. This was the whole list of our New Year's feast.

The taste of our handmade udon was exceptional, thanks to Mrs. T., our neighbour, who had taught us how. Mariko helped her mother and has become quite adept. I hear that some people had planned ahead to store up their New Years foods and there were even those who had made mochi.[7]

Thus the year 1942 has come to a close, at last.

Banished
To a cabin in snow mountains
The year settles down

D I A R Y

March 3, 1943

Clear and sunny. Today is the day of *sekku*, Girls' Day. But in this temporary world a celebration is hard to arrange. A while ago I decided to make dolls for my grandchildren, to celebrate *sekku*. I used rags and anything else I could find. Mrs. Koyama's grandchild is supposed to have her *hatsu-zekku* so I gave as presents my handmade dolls and birds.[8] She was so happy that she came over to say thanks. Here is my *haiku* that I attached to a doll.

Hatsu-zekku
A beaming newborn
Peach blossom

In return Mrs. Koyama gave me a strip of paper with two poems.

Baby crawls
Lovely
Zekku dolls

Remaining snow
Lights up cabin
Spring still young

March 6, 1943

Clear sky. Nothing happening. Temperature is five below. March in Slocan is as clear as crystal.

March 7, 1943

In the afternoon I went to a *haiku* group meeting with my family. I think we all did well. Chisato's poem with a theme of "spring mud" won the highest recognition.

Spring mud
Into the wheel tracks
Cigarette thrown

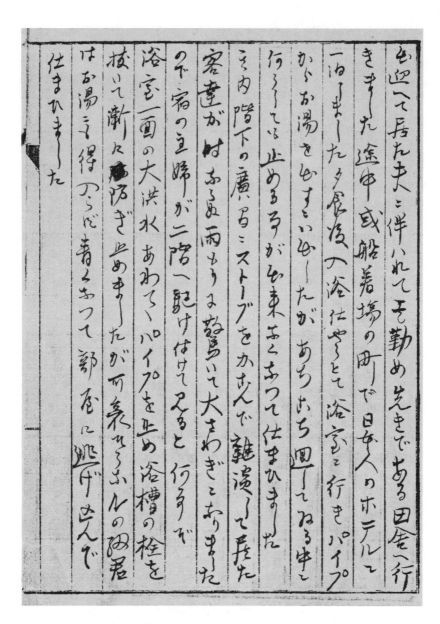

A page from Kaoru Ikeda's journal which she wrote over a two-year period starting in December 1942 and ending in December 1944.

Courtesy of Chisato Tokunaga

One of mine, Chisato's, and one of Mariko's were given high praise. Mine follows:

> Spring mud
> Legs apart
> Edging side to side

The following is Mariko's:

> Tail wagging
> Dog leaps
> Into spring mud

I was especially happy to see Mariko's poem recognized as one of the better ones.

March 13, 1943

It's been raining for days, the snow is now almost all gone. Spring is in the air. The long winter of hibernation is slowly coming to an end. However for us Japanese spring still seems faraway. The other day there was an announcement that the land, houses and other properties in B.C., owned by Japanese would all be disposed by the Custodians. I know there are people whose boats and cars have already been sold. One person whose car cost nearly one thousand dollars, had it sold for seventy-five dollars and after the Custodians took their handling and transportation fees, the man got next to nothing. This situation is causing panic among those with properties.

On the other hand I hear that Canada's shortage of manpower is becoming a serious problem. There are government people who want to send the Japanese to farms in Eastern Canada. They are trying to do it but they can't agree on one policy. The Japanese are sick and tired of the government and the Commission wavering and feel they cannot trust them. As Japanese we are not willing to accept the idea of going East. There is a rumour that the government will use force. They say after the work in the winter those who were working for the Commission now have no jobs to go to. They say that they will never give unemployment relief. This implies that there is no other way than to move East.

So young bachelors, who have few responsibilities, have begun to move. But middle-aged men, with a family to support, well . . . it is not so easy. They are worried about having to do different labour than they are used to. It is almost a year since last spring and we are finally settling into our simple life. And now they are talking about removing us again. So the women here are disturbed and spend a lot of time anxiously discussing what will happen. I also hear rumours that the young people working in the road camps will also be forced to move to sugarbeet farms. I am very worried about my son. Right here my son-in-law will be able to work in the office for the time being, but in the future we don't know what will happen. Chisato is worried.

The Japanese Committee is said to be planning to appeal to the Ottawa government to overturn the decision to dispose of our personal properties. I doubt very much that such an appeal will do anything. Now we are prisoners of the war, living in an enemy country. They will do whatever they want to do. The politicians in the province of British Columbia are determined to uproot the foundations that the Japanese had managed to lay. I pray that the strength of our nation will shine over us one day . . .

In our camp there are disturbing rumours about our young boys. Fifteen- and sixteen-year-old boys are said to have stolen from stores in the town of Slocan and Bay Farm. Among these children, gambling is very popular so they always need money. Most of them come from homes where the parents have given up hope for themselves and their kids. No wonder their kids are wild.

The other day Miss Cox visited us and we had a nice chat. She said under such conditions, many Japanese stopped being real Japanese. I thought we cannot hide the Japanese weaknesses from Miss Cox. Having lived in Japan for forty years, Miss Cox can see through us. I felt ashamed. I really wish that the Japanese would retain their good and moral Japanese ways.

Construction of the school is finished, so children can now start going to school in April.

The other day Chisato made tofu which she learned from Mrs. Kawabata from across the way. It was very delicious. I had believed that we didn't have the necessary ingredients for tofu but according to Mrs. Kawabata we can substitute Epsom salts. Camp life has its own merit. Because we are here we are learning certain ways to survive.

These days the price increases are outrageous. There are shortages of almost everything. The lack of vegetables is especially serious. A cabbage the size of a baby's head costs from thirty to fifty cents, a bunch of celery from fifty to eighty cents, spinach is twenty-five cents a pound, apples sixty cents a dozen, oranges are eighty-five cents a dozen, and canned goods are practically nonexistent.

Now that the snow is gone everybody is working hard to make their own vegetable gardens. Digging gardens in this country is hard because of the stumps, rocks and trees. But everyone works hard, making nice borders from the wood, and the gardens all look pretty. In my family we are also very busy digging and planting gardens. An acquaintance from the town gave me bulbs for various flowers so I decided to make a small flower garden just in front of our house. I found last year's pansies and snapdragons still alive after a long winter, so I transplanted them into my new garden.

September 27, 1943

It's cold in the mornings and evenings. I hear that vegetables were damaged by frost in Bay Farm and Popoff. So everyone is putting cloth sacks and newspapers over their gardens. Since we don't have much in our garden, we don't have to cover it, except the chrysanthemums which are beginning to bloom.

I learned from a friend how to make pickled plums as a substitute for Japanese umeboshi pickles. So we bought green plums. Luckily we have some shiso, red beef-steak plant, leaves planted in the garden which we added to the pickled plums. It is an excellent substitute. Here shiso is very rare, so I gave several friends some of the precious leaves. I hear those without shiso would use beets for red colouring. People made me promise to give them seeds so I will try to extract as many shiso seeds as possible.

Fuki, coltsfoot, is also very precious. People are asking me for even a small root of it. I was told that it is best to replant fuki in the fall and cover it with compost so that next spring good sprouts will come out. I asked my son-in-law to do the job. He found that the roots were strong and long, so I could give some to my friends.

Mariko was accepted at the Slocan high school and is now commuting. There she still gets a correspondence course but being in a school environment is better for her. The Catholic Church opened a high school which many attend, and the Anglican Church just opened a high school too and many of Mariko's friends are now going there. Both schools only go up to grade eleven, so as a twelfth grader Mariko had to go to the Slocan high school.

Our chrysanthemums have small yellow flowers. These are the ones my grandchildren received in New Denver as Easter presents. Thanks to my son-in-law who took good care of them, they are doing well.

Each morning
More in blossom
Garden mums

Hand cut
chrysanthemums
Soaked in perfume

October 4, 1943

Mountain lodge
Leaves drift in
Through morning windows

October 7, 1943

Clear and sunny. Beautiful autumn sky and a pleasant day. Today is the anniversary of my son Ken's death. Chisato cut some chrysanthemums and offered them along with various other things. Everybody seems thoughtful. It is hard to believe, eleven years have already passed.

October 10, 1943

Pouring rain. The rain hasn't stopped since yesterday. I have been sick the last few days. I have a terrible cough and therefore am staying in bed.

October 14, 1943

Clear and sunny. Feeling better I finally got up. The last few days suddenly became cold and this morning the ground was completely frozen and spoiled our garden. Everybody is busy salvaging whatever they can from their gardens. Our chrysanthemums withered. In the afternoon I walked into the mountains for a short walk. Probably because the summer was too dry or too many trees have been cut down the mushrooms are no good this year.

I hear that the Canadian government decided on a policy of "selective service" in which young bachelors are forced to go East for work. These are Canadian-born young people. How can the government treat these Canadians in the same way as they treat us — as enemy aliens? The government deprived them of their simple human and civil rights and herded them off to unfamiliar places. Although stripped of their rights the Japanese Canadian men are still expected to live up to the obligations of being Canadians when the Government sees fit. How unreasonable! I know well that there is no point in resisting but I can't control my anger.

I read in the newspaper that the British, American and Japanese are meeting on a Portuguese island to exchange prisoners of war. I imagine that Mr. and Mrs. T. and others are now happily getting into the Japanese ship.

October 18, 1943

There was a sad incident today. Two men who live in town went into the mountains, beyond the lake, to gather mushrooms. They got lost. One found his way back to town at midnight but the other one did not come back. Early this morning dozens of people went into the mountains to look for him. They found his dead body under a cliff. They guessed that he fell off the cliff in the total darkness. He had a wife and seven children. I felt so sorry for his family.

These days it has been raining and chilly, which doesn't make me feel very good. But today is nice. So in the afternoon I went to visit old Mrs. Sekine to give her white lily bulbs and the fuki roots.

Morning frost
Chrysanthemum flowers
Drooping slightly

Mountain gift
For my hair
Fallen red leaf

November 4, 1943

Today is my sixty-eighth birthday. I just keep on accumulating years without being very useful to others. But I'm grateful that I'm not sick and therefore a burden on everybody.

November 13, 1943

Arranging chrysanthemums
Silently
I celebrate this day

November 18, 1943

Today is Chisato's birthday. Ayako baked a delicious cake for her mother. It was also Naomi's birthday, from across the way, so we took some cake to her.

The Spanish consul came to visit and at the Bay Farm camp had a meeting with the Japanese Committee. According to the consul, Spain is limited to trying to protect Japanese nationals and they are not concerned with Nisei or naturalized Canadians. This statement is caused much agitation among the Japanese here. The Canadian government has taken everything not only from the Japanese nationals but also from the Nisei and the naturalized Canadians. Thus we all ended up together in the interior. But if the Japanese and Spanish governments thrust us aside as Canadians then what will we do? No protection from anybody. Some are upset, some are depressed. It's a big mess.

More thoughtful people say that Japan won't give up on us. It is rather understandable for the Spanish to officially take this position. The Japanese government and the people must know how we are treated by Canada. For instance some Japanese, including Nisei and naturalized Canadians, have already gone back to Japan through prisoner exchange programs. They are sure to have reported what is going on over here.

The Canadian government is so hypocritical. On the one hand they deprive us of the right to be Canadian and on the other they regard us as Canadian when they need our manpower. Their so called selective service is now being challenged by many people so the government are shifting their position and have now begun to allow some young people to work within the province of B.C. More and more young people who are eager to work are going to logging camps. Then again those parents whose sons had been sent to the East are complaining that it's not fair that others are allowed to remain in B.C. to work. I hear that there was an incident where these people with complaints demonstrated to the Commission office making a large scene. I think everything stems from the governments lack of definite direction.

A hastily-built cabin in the Slocan Valley shared by two families
of fourteen people. The kitchen was in the centre. The temperature
in the winter could go down as low as -30° F.

Courtesy of Kotoma Kitagawa

December 7, 1943

Oh the unforgettable day has come around again! Snow was late this year but since yesterday it has been falling. The chill is now definitely in the air. For me it became impossible to go out for even a short time. I spent my day quietly reading and knitting.

December 24, 1943

In the afternoon on this Christmas Eve day we were surprised to see the Mounted Police go into the mountains and come back with a big radio receiver on a sled. We heard that somebody informed the Mounties that Mr. K., who lives above us, had a short wave radio. They raided his house and confiscated the radio. Deep in the mountains without much entertainment would it be so harmful for someone to listen to the radio? I'm shocked at the narrow-mindedness of the Mounties and the existence of a Japanese informant who will sell-out his own people. I cannot help feeling hateful. I feel sorry for Mr. K.

December 25, 1943

As we are already accustomed to this, we erected a small Christmas tree and when the neighbour's kids came over to play we gave them cookies. The roast chicken dinner was delicious. We received many beautiful Christmas cards. These days the children are enjoying opening their mail.

December 28, 1943

In the evening Mariko gave a Christmas party inviting her high school friends. Everybody cheerfully enjoyed themselves until around eleven o'clock.

December 31, 1943

Another humble New Year is upon us. The Inoue family from Popoff gave us precious white radish so I made everyone's favourite dish with it. I also made some *sushi* dishes for New Year's. For the last dinner of the year I made *miso* soup with my homemade *miso* that I opened for the first time. Mariko made a pun saying; "We eat *miso* on the night of *omisoka* [the last day of the year]" So everybody laughed. I thought the *miso* was pretty well made. That made me happy. Well, so much for another year.

I thought
It would be just temporary
In this mountain country
Accumulating another year
As snow deepens

January 25, 1944

For the last two or three days it has been severely cold. This morning
the engine in the generator house stopped and there was a black-out.
The water has also stopped flowing. Chisato went to a nearby water tank
and came back with hot water and with that we prepared our breakfast.
After breakfast Mr. Inoue kindly got some buckets and pots to fetch us
some water.

January 30, 1944

Clear and sunny, very cold. Today there was distribution of the care
packages from Japan at the Bay Farm school. I saw the people from across
the street going with empty buckets to pick up their packages. My
daughter and Tokunaga also went during the morning. One bottle of
soya sauce per person, one pound of tea per family and half a pound of
miso per family.

Reaching out
With compassion
Precious gift
From my native land.

Old country memories
Carried back
With scent of tea

Sitting looking at this gift which has travelled across the world, sent
by my compatriots I can barely restrain my tears, as the memories
well-up. At lunch we gathered to drink some of the tea, appreciating
it's beautiful scent, good quality and rich taste.

At first there were many conflicting opinions as to how to distribute
the care packages. I hear the Committee members spent a lot of time

discussing the possibilities. According to some people these packages were sent as gifts for the Japanese nationals and were not supposed to be distributed to the Nisei and naturalized Canadians. But then others argued that everybody here is herded together as enemy aliens, so we should not discriminate against anybody. People were divided about whether to distribute to each individual or each household. They even debated whether a small baby should be considered as a person to receive goods. At the end they concluded that even a baby should be treated with equal rights.

It was announced that the empty soya sauce barrels would be sold. We wanted to buy one but there were already too many other people who also wanted to buy, so we all ended up drawing lots. Fortunately we were lucky enough to buy a barrel. The care packages were distributed to every camp where Japanese Canadians have been relocated. There was an article in the *The New Canadian* about the trouble concerning the distribution of the care packages. A group of young Nisei in Eastern Canada insisted that they were Canadians with no relationship whatsoever to Japan. To distribute care packages to them, they argued, was an insult to them as Canadians. Using strong words they refused the package and again protested to the Ottawa government asking to be recognized as Canadian citizens. This appeal was signed by several people who were lead by Obata and Tanaka. For an old person like myself this behaviour was far beyond my comprehension.

Those young people born in this country grew up and received their education here. Now they have settled in the East and are trying their best to be accepted as true Canadians. Considering all this, their actions are understandable. But the real problem is that even though they repeatedly try to prove their loyalty to Canada, Canadians are such traditionally strong racists that they refuse them equal treatment. For the time being because of the wartime shortage of man power, Canada is trying to make the best use of Nikkei labour, but when the time comes they will flip their attitudes to the other side. We have seen Canada's true nature through our recent experiences. What is democracy? Who can talk about it? Who has the right to accuse Japan of invading other countries? Isn't Britain the champion invader? The last several centuries of British history is full of invasion after invasion. Since they can be neither Japanese nor Canadian, I wonder what the future of the Nisei youth will be? Deprived of civil rights these young people are in a sad situation. I just hope that their efforts will lead to a positive solution.

April, 1944

Easter has passed and it is getting warmer everyday. Everybody is busy with their gardens. Hiroko-san's mother who fell suddenly ill, died in the Grand Forks hospital. We received Hiroko's telegram. They will cremate her in New Denver and then hold a memorial service in a local church. My family members will attend.

May, 1944

I've been seriously ill since midnight of the twelfth. The doctor came to examine me and said I had to go to the hospital. So right away I got into the doctor's car, accompanied by Chisato, and went to the hospital. I was told that I had an ulcer of the intestine. It was very painful and I was often nauseous. I couldn't swallow anything, including medicine. They had to inject me with the medicine and put an intravenous in my arm for nutrition. For a while they said I was in critical condition, but after four days the pain began to lessen and I was able to take in a small amount of medicine and orange juice. The doctor assured me that I would recover. Chisato and others have been very concerned and have been taking good care of me. I had many friends visiting me everyday. My son Arimoto was informed of my condition by telegram and he came from his camp.

June, 1944

After nearly a month the pain finally ceased, although I felt very weak. Finally the doctor allowed me to go home and rest. So at the beginning of June I left the hospital. Relieved, Arimoto went to work in a logging camp.

I heard that Hiroko-san had an operation for appendicitis in the New Denver hospital. I feel very sorry that she became sick so soon after losing her mother. I pray for a quick recovery.

July, 1944

For a month or so I rested, got well and was able to walk around outside. While I was sick the snow melted and the mountain turned green. The garden was lush and full of vegetables. I don't want to fall ill again so I am going to be very careful. I feel sorry that my illness caused a lot of worry and trouble to my family and friends. To all those people who gave me get-well presents, I distributed Pyrex cups as tokens of my appreciation.

August, 1944

We were all surprised to hear that Grandmother Inoue from Popoff was admitted to the hospital. Chisato ran to the hospital but she couldn't see Grandmother Inoue because she had been placed in a critical ward. It was hard to believe she was so well when she came to visit me in the hospital. A week or so later when I heard that she was able to have visitors, I cut some flowers from my garden and went to visit her. She was very gaunt and pale, but I was glad to see that she was no longer in critical condition. While I was there I figured I should look in on some other people including Mrs. Yamashita who was having her baby, and Emiko-san who had been my roommate when I was in hospital.

Although it is still very hot, I take walks in the mountains to pick huckleberries. I made jam out of them, a couple of times. Since the Matsubayashi family moved to Eastern Canada Mariko is separated from her best friends and feels sad. These days increasing numbers of people are moving to the East. The authorities are said to have a policy to amalgamate some of the camps in order to save energy and costs to the Commission. The Sandon Camp has been closed and I feel sorry for those who were kicked out of the place where they lived for two years, only to be shipped to another camp. The majority moved to New Denver and many were resettled in Slocan, Popoff, and Bay Farm. The shelter where the Matsubayashis lived was taken over by the Miyake family.

There were also some people moved from Greenwood to Lemon Creek and there is also a rumour that the camp in Kaslo will be closed. I hear that the people will then be moved to Tashme.

September, 1944

One Sunday I went to see a farm show full of flowers and vegetables at the Bay Farm school. There was a good crowd and a lot of good participants. Besides many kinds of vegetables there are also pots of flowers all very well done and impressive. The best of them won prizes going from third to first. Among our friends Mr. Suzuki got two second prizes for his enormous pumpkin and green pepper. The first prizes went to people from Popoff and Lemon Creek but in any case I was so impressed by the hard work it must have taken to create these beautiful things in a wild land filled with roots and rocks. Before I left the show I had a chat with Suzuki-san and he gave me some beautiful tomatoes, saying that he could have placed these in the competition. It was hard to believe that he is an amateur farmer.

Last night our garden was trampled by calves. This morning I went out to inspect it and there were big hoof marks everywhere. I found carrots, radishes, and Chinese cabbage eaten. I hear that our neighbours' gardens also received a lot of damage. Although they were behind a log fence the cows either stepped over it, or if it was too high, pushed it over. Well what can we do?

November, 1944

This fall the mushrooms have been plentiful in the back mountains. So I have been enjoying my walks everyday. Last Sunday Tokunaga and Chisato went hiking over the waterfall and found several precious *matsutake* mushrooms. They were tiny but had very good scent. Later they told me a story. On the top of the mountain, Tokunaga sat down on a rock to rest and have a smoke when I.-san passed by. He found some *matsutake* just under Tokunaga's legs and took them for himself. We all laughed at Tokunaga who hadn't even noticed the mushrooms right near his feet. We cooked *matsutake* rice, our first dish in many years. Of course we enjoyed it.

There are rumours that the mountain on the other side of the lake has many *matsutake* mushrooms and many people are hurrying over there to find them. From my neighbourhood there are people who came back with a big sack full of the mushrooms. They shared them with everybody and as a result we got two or three good mushrooms. To get to this mountain one has to row for three hours across the lake, then climb several miles towards the peak, so not just anybody can go mushroom gathering.

November 4, 1944

Today is my birthday. In the morning everybody wished me a happy birthday. Because I had been ill I was afraid that I would not be able to live until this birthday but I am grateful to have made it.

November 11, 1944

An exhibition of chrysanthemums was held at the Bay Farm school. Fortunately the weather was good, so I decided to go for a little exercise. The rest of my family had gone yesterday. There were many pots of various colours. A lot of energy and effort had been put into the flowers. On one wall there were fifteen or sixteen *tanka* poems with the theme being chrysanthemums. The calligraphy teacher, Mr. Miyake, copied the poems out. The following poem of mine was among them.

Desolate garden
Of our temporary home
Nobly
Pointing to eternity
The fragrance of white chrysanthemums.

In October the weather was good and warm. The chrysanthemums are doing very well in our garden and we cut and give them to our friends. But as November began, chilly rainy days continued and most of the garden things withered in the cold and rain. Most people weren't ready for this because the weather had been so warm in October.

A log cabin in Bay Farm caught fire and three families were forced out into the cold . . . As winter approaches I feel so sorry for them. The Japanese Committee (Hakko-kai) decided to take up a collection to help out the families. In the meantime, acquaintances of each family, have been donating small amounts of goods. One of the older couples moved into the building across the way. They had lost everything so we are collecting kitchen utensils, old clothes, shoes, and so on.

November 20, 1944

At night the first snowfall of the year arrived. It came down for only about two hours. Since then it's been snowing and then melting, snowing and then melting. The road was washed out under mud and water, but thanks to the weather the air is good and clear.

November 30, 1944

Arimoto came to join us because his camp has closed. We heard that his camp was infested by bed bugs and we were afraid that he'd bring some of them with him. They put all his belongings into a small hut and the Commission's sanitation department disinfected everything. On top of that we had to boil sheets and other things just to be sure. The building across the way had been complaining that there were bedbugs but our house is isolated, and this has spared us from having the same problem.

December 7, 1944

This day is back again. It has been three long years since Pearl Harbour. What is happening in my native country? The Americans have been joyfully boasting of the bombing of Tokyo. But also I hear that Japan is doing very well on many battle fronts which the Americans haven't talked about. I can only pray for good results. The news from radios and newspapers that we get access to are full of propaganda. The difference between reality and propaganda is now hard to distinguish. I cannot believe everything that is reported. Because we cannot hear the news from Japan we are in a constant state of anxiety.

S L O C A N   H A I K U   C L U B

Some poems from a meeting one early spring. The authors are unknown.

[*Themes: Early Spring, Spring Thaw*]

Grass on the riverbank
Left flat and disorderly
Spring is still shallow

•

Early spring
In time with the sunshine
Children are dancing

•

Thinking far
While gazing on
Early spring snow

•

Balmy weather
Lake surface swelling
Spring thaw

•

Strolling in the field
Soft pathway
Young spring

•

Bright mountain
Trees embracing
Early spring sun

•

Spring thaw
Nearly bursting
Cow's udder

NOTES

1. *Mame* has two meanings: "good health" and "beans." The T.'s served the bean dish to wish them good health.

2. The five family members were the author herself, her daughter Chisato, Chisato's husband Tokunaga, and their daughters Junko and Mariko.

3. *Sun*, the Japanese "inch" is equal to 1.19 inches.

4. *Matsutake* mushrooms which grow in pine woods are a favourite Japanese delicacy.

5. *Hakko*, meaning the whole world, evokes Japan's mission of uniting the world under its leadership. It was a key propaganda word in wartime Japan.

6. *Kuri-kinton*, sweet made with chestnut traditionally prepared for the New Year celebration.

7. *Mochi*, a pounded rice cake is the most important food and symbol of the New Year.

8. *Hatsu-zekku* or first *zekku* is a celebration for girls on their first March 3rd following birth. The celebration for boys is on their first May 5th. Both are considered important rites of passage.

Footsteps:
Autobiography
of a Socialist

Genshichi Takahashi

Footsteps: Autobiography of a Socialist

GENSHICHI TAKAHASHI

Editor's Introduction

"I am a socialist," Genshichi Takahashi told me the first time we met, as if he was angry. This was his way of introducing himself. I hope that it may be possible to review Japanese Canadian history through his socialist point-of-view and that it may even be possible to reconsider the concept of socialism in the context of Japanese Canadian history.

Genshichi Takahashi was born in 1904 in Shiga Prefecture, Japan. He immigrated to Canada in 1922 when he was seventeen. While working in the sawmills of British Columbia he studied on his own and became involved in the union movement. He became a member of the radical Japanese youth league which was eventually purged from the Japanese Labour Union led by the well-known journalist and labour unionist, Etsu Suzuki. Following the hard times of the Depression, he worked as a shoe repairman, food retailer, and food wholesaler. In 1942 he was forced to leave Vancouver and lost his business and the house that he had built himself. After working in a road camp in the interior of British Columbia he subsequently joined his family on a sugarbeet farm in Alberta.

Takahashi, along with his Nisei wife Mika and their only child Ken, were among about four thousand Nikkei who would spend the war years in the Prairie Provinces labouring mainly on sugarbeet projects set up by the British Columbia Security Commission.

In 1945, convinced of the approaching defeat of Japan, he took his family to Montreal to begin life anew. After the war he worked for a shoe repair shop and a fruit store. Later he owned and managed a rooming house while his wife worked in a textile factory. During this period Takahashi played a leading role in the creation of a consumer's cooperative in Montreal's Japanese community. Genshichi Takahashi and his wife Mika still live in Montreal, spending as much time as possible tending their prize-winning garden.

As he explains in his Preface, Takahashi wrote this memoir at the urging of his cousin who regarded the author as the only one who could record their family history. The complete work therefore contains many anecdotes depicting relationships among family members and relatives, often those of a conflicting nature. Although most of these stories are not contained in this book, the reader should note that some of the family problems stemmed from the fact that the author was perceived by the family to be an undesirable man with radical ideas. In his memoir, however, we see that along with his strong political views he was, nevertheless, a man who committed himself to some traditional values. He was determined not to get married before a bank account was established for his parents large enough for them to retire on. Takahashi also played a leading role as conciliator in his clan to settle serious problems. Despite being an atheist, he would pray in front of his family's ancestral altar. Genshichi and Mika Takahashi had been members of the Nikkei Buddhist Church. Regarding this apparent contradiction he explains that it is only because the people in the church are all good friends and not because he wishes to enter heaven!

Reflecting yet another face of this complex man, Takahashi was a hard-working labourer and a competent businessman. He taught himself socialism but he also had a good understanding of the capitalist system. He had almost established himself as a successful vegetable wholesaler when the Canadian government took away his business. His talents as an entrepreneur were demonstrated again during the Alberta days when, with the help of native people of the region, he grew vegetables successfully and profitably instead of working in the sugarbeet fields as most Japanese Canadians were doing. Takahashi's postwar efforts for the Nikkei consumer's cooperative in Montreal can be interpreted as a combination of his business skills and his socialist ideas.

P R E F A C E

My cousin had been encouraging me to write my autobiography, but I felt that I was not a person worthy of an autobiography so I never listened to him seriously. Last spring my cousin wrote to me insisting, "While you are alive I can always ask you things. But since you are getting old I want you to please write something and leave it for my sake. If you don't feel like writing about yourself, you could write something in the form of a novel." At that time I still thought I hadn't done anything worth writing about.

One day when friends were visiting, they mentioned that one of their acquaintances in Winnipeg, who is over eighty years old, was writing about his own life experiences. That reminded me of my cousin's letter. For the first time I thought that maybe I too should do it. Well, where should I begin? No, no. I don't want to get involved in something like this. I left it at that.

Some time later I realized that my interest in this subject remained. After all, I thought, I was born and have lived this long. I have lived my own life, not anybody else's. I am not trying to write for somebody else; I am trying to gaze into my own life, disentangling all the old and weather-beaten threads to give some kind of shape to this reflection. It will be too late once I lose the use of my eyes and hands. So I began to dig into my memory without any intention of having someone else read it. I began with childhood which I think must be the clearest and strongest memory for most people.

When I finished writing this autobiography I entitled it "Footsteps." The process was not as slow as I thought. While writing I felt that I was immersed in those places and times again, walking through my life again. It was only after I finished writing that I saw my life as a series of footsteps into the past. I tried to be as faithful as possible to the facts, however it is possible that my memory errs about things which happened a long time ago.

My feet are small, therefore my footsteps are also small. I grew up in poverty so my feet could not grow big. But I'm glad I didn't step on or kick other people around with big feet. I'm glad that I have small feet.

Genshichi Takahashi, May 1982

Along with his strong political views, Genshichi Takahashi was committed to some traditional values. In this pre-war photograph from Japan, the calligraphy states that an offering was received for a relative's funeral from Genshichi Takahashi of Canada.

Courtesy of Genshichi Takahashi

M E M O I R

Childhood

I was born in the thirty-seventh year of the Meiji Period. As I think about that I wonder how I managed to survive to this old age. In the developed countries where we live, the standard of living has become much higher and life expectancy has become longer, but there are many, many people on the same earth living in miserable and inhumane conditions. Whenever I think of those people I feel a pain in my heart. I don't want this to be seen as a shallow sentiment of humanistic sympathy, rather, thinking about these people makes my childhood memories well up from the bottom of my heart, bringing me that pain.

My native village, beside Lake Biwa, eked out a bare subsistence in agriculture and fishing. The villagers were tenants working on the rice fields owned by a tiny handful of landlords. At that time the Yodo River waterway which later controlled the water level of Lake Biwa had not been completed. During severe rainstorms the Inugami River, north of the village, overflowed its banks and flooded fields, farms and houses. Villagers whose homes were washed away would build a small shack to shelter themselves. These small shacks would be washed away again. It was a miserable life. By contrast, landlords lived in large, sturdy houses. The houses and yards were protected by high storm walls and iron gates which hid them from view.

The house where I was born, as I vaguely remember it, was not really a house but a small one-room shack. It had one small window which let in the light from outside and there was a well in the front yard. Straw mats were placed on top of a layer of small, smooth pebbles taken from the shore. That's where my younger brother and I were born.

In 1908, when I was three-years-old, my father went to Canada to work for a Vancouver store. My mother, brother, myself and my father's mother stayed behind. My grandmother died at the end of the same year. Lacking even farming tools, my father had been supporting my family by buying fish at the market and taking them to the city of Hikone to sell. When he was gone, mother had to feed us somehow. It was the beginning of my mother's long, long struggle.

The store in Vancouver also seemed to be in hard times and could not pay my father even the small salary stipulated in the contract. I imagine that he was very worried since he himself was barely surviving and could not send money home. He would promise in his letters to send money by giving up his love of drinking, but he never managed to keep that promise. In order to console himself in his despair he began to drink crude home-made *doburoku sake* that an acquaintance gave him out of pity. Then, hoping to multiply the little money he had, he began to frequent Chinese gambling parlours.

For thirteen years father did not send much money home and he wasted his days by drinking and gambling. But it was not his fault. I would always try to explain that to my brother. I would not say it was good that mother had to suffer so much but that we should not hate father for that. It is rather understandable that a man alone in a foreign land without any consolation would find some joy in drinking and excitement in gambling.

Father's thoughts did not reach too far because he did not have any education. But he was not to be blamed for that. The real root of our suffering and father's suffering was poverty. It was not father who was bad but the time that was bad. If we thought that by learning from him we could avoid ending up like him, then we could even be thankful for his sacrifice. This was what I tried to explain to my brother.

In order to bring us up, mother had to go through hardships that were beyond description. My mother's family was also landless and poor. She would help them with farming chores to earn some rice to feed us. But she needed some cash so she did whatever extra work she found: sorting scallion bulbs, shelling and boiling tiny shellfish, pulling in fish nets. We would go along with her when we could. But since day labour in the fields began early in the morning and did not finish until late at night, my brother and I would wait for mother's return in the darkness of the house. There were no electric lights then. Other families had table lamps but our house only had candles and lanterns. My mother would say, "Fire is dangerous," and not let us light them. I remember that on dry nights, when we knew where she was working, the two of us would walk along the dark paths through the fields to meet her.

When I began elementary school we were living in a shed, even smaller than the shack where I was born. There was no window and once the door was closed it was pitch black. There wasn't even a well, so we had to get water from our neighbour.

When I think of my mother who brought us up in such hardship, tears fill my eyes. When nobody is around I cry like a baby.

Across the Ocean

When I was sixteen father came back to Japan like Urashima-taro.[1] He was the man who had left me when I was three and whose face I remembered only from photographs. I had no education beyond elementary school and my family was poor. Even as a child I thought that I would go to work in a big city or else, if possible, go to Canada. I asked father if he had brought us our passports to America. He said curtly that he had his own passport, not ours, and would not be able to get them either. 'I don't know if it's possible or not, but I would like to try to go back with you anyway,' I said. But he didn't listen to me seriously.

In those days there was a rumour in our village that six or seven young boys managed to immigrate to Canada using other people's papers. Even though our hamlet had sent so many people to Canada and the United States that it was nicknamed *Amerika Mura* or America Village, it was becoming harder and harder to send more because of restrictive immigration policies.

But I did not give up. Once I had decided, I would try my best. If I gave up before trying I would never succeed at anything anyway. I would try, believing in the possibility. I persisted. I was sixteen.

Finally I obtained the passports against everyone's expectations. Father looked incredulous, wondering how I had done it.

In 1922 I sailed out of Yokohama with my father and brother, each of us with a valid passport. It was a five thousand ton freighter called *Hawaii-Maru*. We slept on beds which stuck out of the wall like shelves. I was seventeen.

When I left Japan I promised my mother that I would work hard for three years or so and return with some money. But things didn't turn out as I thought they would, and now, some sixty years later, Japan has become a country foreign to me.

Here is one of the unforgettable experiences of my life. Although during the first few days on the ship people were shy with one another, they became closer as the days passed. "Which *ken* do you come from?[2] Where are you heading?" In the small, enclosed space of the ship people got to know one another quickly. Since it was a freighter there were no recreation facilities.

Two or three dining room tables were constantly occupied with gamblers. Father was among them. I figured this was the reason why he hadn't been able to send money to us before.

One day one of the gambling regulars came to sit with us on our bed. He said things like this: "Where are you from? Where are you going? How lucky your father is to have good sons like you . . . But you boys, don't you ever forget this — don't take up gambling in Vancouver even if your father doesn't quit. I myself wasted my life with gambling. Unlike your father, I don't have a son or a wife. I'm all alone.

What began as a harmless little game led me into the serious world of gambling. Now I know no other way of living. I'm a waste, human garbage, making a living from the money that I take by cheating at the tables while other people work. It is a shame but there's no use regretting it now.

Now that you are entering the real world I don't want you to repeat my mistake. My destination is Seattle so I will not see you again, but please do not forget what I said. Live an honest life."

The man patted my head and then left us. With his mustache and stately stature and manner he looked like a fine gentleman or a university professor. He seemed close to sixty years old. He might have gone to the United States as a student when he was young.

In the second week after landing, the Japanese foreman of a sawmill in West Vancouver gave me a job doing yardwork. I got seventeen-and-a-half cents per hour. There were quite a few Japanese workers. A month or so later I left that place and went with Father to Skeena to fish for salmon. This work was unbearably hard for my young body. For five days, without sleeping, we rowed upstream against the strong current, put the nets in the water, rowed upstream and pulled them out again, over and over.

Skeena is a place well-known for rain. It rained almost everyday. Working on the wet boat in a rain coat and high rubber boots was so hard that I thought I was shortening my life. Hemorrhoids, which I had ever since elementary school, were also plaguing me again.

But there was another reason which made me firmly decided not to go back to that place again. It was the atmosphere. And I don't mean the physical air we breathe. In the fishermen's camp there were many people from the Shiga prefecture, most of whom were honest and nice men. But in the neighbouring camp there were the ones called *Shikina goro*[3] who only worked during the summer salmon season and hung around the boathouse the rest of the year. Those single men would get drunk and fight with knives. Their violence and destructiveness, the likes of which I had never seen before, made me tremble.

As the salmon season neared the end and there was more leisure time, the gambling began. The gamblers would arrive from Vancouver to swindle the fishermen's money. Three men or so would form a team, move into a camp and open up gambling tables.

The team of gamblers pretended they had no schemes but they would take turns lying down near the table to rest their eyes. There was always one resting. The fishermen were up all night gambling without rest so naturally they always lost in the end. But they didn't understand this. It was the same story every year. There were many workers who lost all the money that they had earned through back breaking labour to those parasites who just played around in Vancouver waiting for the season to come. Fishermen who didn't stay in Skeena lost their money on the way out to gamblers who worked on the boats.

Just as some people are alcohol addicts, these people were gambling addicts. My father was one of them, I think. I remember that when I was still in Japan he would send letters every year saying that if the year's catch was good he would come home. I also remember that a letter would follow saying the catch was bad and he wouldn't be able to come home.

I never went back to Skeena. Father had to give up fishing because I wouldn't help him. The following year was said to be a good year for the fishermen. Father was envious and angry but I didn't feel any regret whatsoever.

Father

The three of us got a job at Hastings sawmill and worked there until the mill was closed down. I don't remember exactly when the company closed. I guess it was something like 1927 or '28. That huge sawmill, owned by English people, was built on land that the native Indians had been cheated out of for a paltry sum of money. Somebody told me that the Indians came to clean the offices once a year as an expression of gratitude for the money they were given every year. That land was sold years later for millions of dollars.

Canada was once Indian land. English people came, kicked out the natives and established a British colony. I remember that when I came from Japan I saw some mountains with all the trees burnt. I thought that there had been forest fires, but later I read in a book of British

Columbia history that the English people used to burn the forest to force away the natives and wipe them out. Today Canada is believed to be white man's country. French Canadians believe that Quebec is their country and are strong with their nationalism. But as a matter of fact, this Canada is neither their's nor English Canadians'. The real owners are those Indians who have been living in Canada since ancient times. If they had had one unified government instead of separate chiefdoms, Canada would be a legitimate, independent Indian nation.

At Hastings sawmill I sorted logs that rolled down the conveyor. I earned twenty-seven-and-a-half cents per hour. I worked forty-four hours per week plus two hours of overtime four evenings per week. Over and above that I went to clean the mill every Sunday for half a day. There was no extra pay for overtime like there is today.

In my native hamlet of Hassaka there were only old people and children, but almost no young couples or sons of working age. Many of them were actually in Canada. The men were mainly working for sawmills. They would come home with firewood on their shoulders. Women worked for white families as domestics and would bring home old clothes and shoes. They worked hard and lived frugally, trying to save some money. On Sundays they would go fishing for their meals. They would send whatever money they managed to save to Japan, while they lived in cheap housing at seven or ten dollars per month.

More than a thousand people were here from our village. Those from the Shigaken area were often from our village. There were people who joked that anywhere you go you would run into Chinese people and people from our village. The money they so frugally saved was sent to Japan, mostly to build new houses there. A fine house built in the village was a symbol of success. They seemed to believe that a better house would increase a person's value, so they competed to build fine houses.

Father continued to get drunk and go to Chinese gambling parlours. Sometimes we couldn't pay the rent of seventeen dollars and fifty cents for the boden (boarding house). As soon as he received a paycheque from the sawmill he would go to Maekawa's store to cash the cheque, go drinking and then gambling. When he lost at gambling he had no money to pay even for food, so until he got paid two weeks later I always had to pay for him.

I would often tell Father, "If you were not working I would pay for your food, but you better pay at least for your own food since you are working so hard every day. As you know, I'm working even on Sundays because I want to save ten thousand yen so you and mother can live in peace after retirement before I settle down. Papa, I'm not counting on your money nor on the money my brother earns . . ."

I was always telling myself that if I was not strong enough I would repeat my father's life. What excuse would I have then for my mother who suffered so much to raise me? This thought steered the course of my life.

When my father was sober he was an honest and hardworking man. But with alcohol he became another person. He always took twenty dollars to go to the Chinese gambling parlours. When he lost his money he would go to his friend's place, borrow twenty dollars and return to the gambling parlours. I knew where he would go to borrow money and as soon as I found out I would go to pay back the money. The guy told me kindly, "I feel sorry for you kids, but you know how your dad is when he's drunk . . ." But I felt sorry for that guy.

I was slow to reach my goal of ten thousand yen. But after a while a new law passed and the minimum wage became fifty cents. This was a big step toward my goal. At the end of the year (1924) we moved to a cottage on Heatley, where the rent was seven dollars, and began to cook our own meals. It was a small apartment with three rooms lined up from the front to the back. We shared the outside toilet with the next door neighbours. (The reason why we left the boarding house was because I felt sorry for the people in the other rooms when my father came home drunk late on Saturdays and Sundays).

Discovering Socialism

There was no time for me to go out and have a good time since I was working even on Sundays. I spent my spare time reading magazines such as Fuji and Yuben. I had never read magazines before I came to Canada.

One time there was a sawmill strike in Vancouver. Japanese workers were accused of being scabs by *hakujin*, the white people. The newspaper reported that there was a big fight between the strikers and those who went to work.

Japanese newspapers attacked the strikers as Reds, saying that they were under the command of Russian Bolsheviks. Today nobody would equate strikers with Reds and Russians, but fifty or sixty years ago it was commonplace and there were a lot of people who believed such accusations. Words like 'socialism' and 'Bolshevik' frightened people as much as evil things like murder, arson, rape, and robbery.

Since I had grown up in Japan, I also blindly believed that the emperor was our god and that I must love my country and be loyal to it. Without knowing what socialism really meant, I just felt it was something awful and frightening and believed that socialists were traitors who would lead Japan to ruin.

I don't know exactly how it began. A small doubt sprouted in my mind. I began to wonder if it was true that socialism was evil and strikes were a Russian conspiracy. Socialists were everywhere in the world. They were arrested, jailed and persecuted. I wondered what kind of people they could be if such persecution couldn't change their minds.

It was a small sprout of doubt. I remembered reading somewhere that to ask why and how is the driving force of progress. Progress in science also grows out of these questions. Without these questions yesterday would remain yesterday forever.

They say socialism is bad, but how is it bad, I wondered. To call it bad because people call it bad is no more than dogs barking. Alright, I thought, I am going to study socialism and after learning what it is I'm going to decide. To study something is not necessarily to believe it. Knowledge is important . . . In Japan, even to know was illegal.

So far so good. But at that time I couldn't read English. My ability to read Japanese was elementary. Even if there were books, they would be too difficult for someone who had barely finished elementary school.

I stopped buying *Yuben* and tried *Chuokoron*.[4] In those days *Chuokoron* was read by an elite group and was not a popular magazine like it is today. No wonder I couldn't understand it at first. There were so many technical words plus there were many words censored with a row of X's. It was out of the question to ask somebody for help. I just read the same thing over and over again.

I was reckless enough to get involved in a magazine like this just to learn about socialism. But persistence can be a powerful thing. As I read it bit by bit I began to understand the articles, although when there were many X's I couldn't read it, but I could guess the hidden parts from the context. Such as, XXXX (communism), XX (revolution).[5]

I graduated from *Chuokoron* and began reading *Kaizo*. Radical leftists of the time, such as Yamakawa Hitoshi, Sakai Toshihiko, Arahata Kanson, Katayama Sen and Sano Manabu were contributing to this magazine. I also began to read a political magazine called *Taiyo*.[6]

I wonder how much time it took me altogether to discover socialism all by myself. Today in society there are two classes; those who have and those who have not. Those who have are the ones who create the government, laws, the police, the court and the army and use them to maintain themselves. Furthermore, they also use education, culture and religion as tools of domination . . . If workers stop working even for a day darkness will fall upon the world. We are the ones who make the world live. We are the core of society and the country. I began to understand these things. We have to create a country, not for a handful of rich, but for the well-being of the great majority of people. I came to understand the reason why the police hated socialism like an evil and tried to repress it. At last I came to see the roots of the dreadful poverty that we had suffered. I felt that by knowing the truth I wouldn't have to fear any persecution. Many predecessors have been massacred and become martyrs, but these people did not die for nothing. My own power is small but I am determined to travel along this path until I die. This is my belief. To believe or not is one's free will.

Sad Weekends

Moving out of the boarding house I now had to cook, wash clothes and clean the house. These things were never much of a burden for me but what I found most annoying was that every weekend father got drunk on the *doburoku*, became a nuisance, and got into fights with my brother.

Father would go out and come back very late completely drunk. I would take off his clothes and put him in bed but after a while he would get up and piss in a corner of the room. I tried to catch him as he got up so I could take him to the toilet outside. But I don't know how many times he slipped past me. In those days there was no hot water. Half crying, I had to wipe up the urine over and over again with cold water.

They said Saturday night was fun for young people. But I was sad when the weekend approached. I would stay in bed reading books, waiting for father to come back drunk. Sometimes I had to go and fetch him from somebody's house. I couldn't sleep soundly those nights. When I felt really miserable I would remember mother's hardships.

Not only on Saturdays and Sundays when I waited for father, but also on other nights, I read books in bed. It was usual for me to read until two or three o'clock in the morning. During the three years on Heatley I developed double vision. I learned later this was caused by reading under the light bulb which dangled above me to one side.

These days reading makes me sleepy but in those days I could read a thin book in a night. I would remember what was written in the book just as if I was a printer typesetting the text. It was all thanks to reading that I could later participate in debates as an equal with those of higher education. And one more thing; it is in a way thanks to my father that I could devote myself to reading.

After Hastings mill was closed down my brother and I moved to False Creek where there was a small sawmill. Father stopped working completely. After a while we found out that our paycheques couldn't be cashed. When we went to complain to the company we were told to just wait a little longer and everything would be worked out. Eventually I had three bad cheques. We told them that until these cheques could be cashed we wouldn't work. Thus twelve or thirteen Japanese workers began a strike.

While on strike we heard rumours that the Nihonjin-kai[7] had approached the company offering to recruit new workers for the company. We tried to find out if this was true. The Nihonjin-kai was at odds with the Japanese Labour Union so it was possible that they would think strikes were not good for the Japanese. We decided to go to the office of the Nihonjin-kai to find out. Mr. F. was the secretary. I had worked as a partner with him in a sawmill, but now I was not in a position to exchange greetings. I explained to him the reason we were on strike. I told him, "If the association helps replace workers, these cheques that we earned with our labour will become garbage. But the real problem is not just that. Those Japanese who begin to work after us will eventually face the same problems. Why does the Nihonjin-kai act against the welfare of the Japanese workers?" Mr. F. became pale and insisted that he didn't know anything about that. He told us to go talk to Mr. K., the interpreter and notary.

We left and went to Mr. K.'s office on Dunlevy. I repeated the same thing. "I have no information about this," he said. I said, "There's no way that you can know nothing about this since we were sent to you from the association." His condescending and insulting attitude upset me. "Stop acting innocent," I shouted at him, "Stop acting innocent, you parasite. As long as you are making money you don't give a damn about your fellow men!" He was afraid but he said, bluffing, "Get out of here or I'll call the police." We said we were not afraid of the police. In fact we would be glad if this whole thing got written up in the newspaper and became known to the public. "Call the police if you want," I insisted. But he would not pick up the phone.

Later we got help from a Labour Union legal advisor and had the company property seized. Finally we managed to get the full amount owed to us. According to the lawyer, the owner of the company had done similar things in the past; he did not believe that Japanese people could fight back like we had done. He had hoped to keep on bilking his workers.

The Japanese Labour Union and the Youth League

The youth section had already been established within the Labour Union before I became a member. I soon found that the youth group and the union leaders were not getting along well. A main issue at the board meetings was the management of the Minshu (the People's Daily). The following explains the complicated background of this situation. The Japanese community of the time was divided by the rivalry between the Nihonjin-kai and the Labour Union. On the one hand, the Nihonjin-kai was backed by the Imperial Consulate and functioned as a Japanese agency with exclusive rights to handle such procedures as passports, re-entry, family sponsorship, employment, deposit receipts, etc. Crooked notaries, concession hunters, and other influential men got together in the association and enjoyed the profits. Because of its privileged standing applicants had to pay three dollars to the association as a handling fee. Both merchant and farmer associations had to deal carefully with the Nihonjin-kai.

On the other hand, the Labour Union attracted relatively educated and more progressive people.[8] Although it was called the Labour Union they did not understand what the term labour movement really meant. There were many workers who entered the union only because they felt good to see the leader Suzuki Etsu come from Japan to attack the Consul's arrogance and expose various injustices in the Nihonjin-kai.

Originally Suzuki became known in Japan as a bourgeois democratic writer and had nothing to do with socialism or the labour movement. Then he became involved with the well-known woman writer Tamura

Toshiko. Suzuki left his wife and came to Canada to work for the *Tairiku Nippo*. Tamura, who was married as well, later joined Suzuki in Canada and they thus created a home.[9]

The Labour Union's first official organ was called *Rodo Shuho*[10] but was later renamed *Minshu* and began to be published daily. Suzuki was the main editor.[11] This was the third daily newspaper in the small Vancouver Japanese community. Financing the newcomer *Minshu* was naturally hard. This was why the board of the Labour Union was always discussing fundraising. From the beginning the young activists had been against the *Minshu*. Their contention was that the paper was supposed to serve as a tool to propagate the union's position and that it was not necessary to overtax the union in order to increase the circulation. By pushing in that direction, the youth argued, the Labour Union would become a "union for the paper" and it would become vulnerable because it would have to take money from whoever gave it. Even the things which necessitate criticism from the point of view of the labour movement and working class would have to be overlooked, like corruption and betrayal. Forgetting its mission to serve the welfare of the workers, its own daily maintenance became the Labour Union's only objective.

One year the conflict between the *Nihonjin-kai* and the Labour Union became intensified for some reason. Consequently, the Merchant's Association which had many representatives on the board of the *Nihonjin-kai* passed the motion that their member stores would remove all advertisements from the *Minshu*. Without this income the newspaper would not be able to continue; it was in serious trouble. It was at this point that the leader Suzuki came up with the idea of the People's Co-op which would not only compensate the losses but would allow the Labour Union to get even with the merchants. In the *Minshu*, Suzuki urged union members to buy shares of fifty dollars to establish a store. The co-op was to open at a store on Powell Street where I would run a fruit and vegetable wholesale business years later.

Both my friend U. and I were leaders of the Youth League and, at the same time, executive members of the Labour Union. By this time the union's youth section had been transformed into the Youth League and the conflict had come to express itself as the one between Suzuki and the Youth League. The union president, S., was then still a member of the Youth League and there were more hidden members of the league among the union officials. The league was no longer a subordinate part of the union but was virtually an independent organization. Some people who were disappointed with the union came into the league. There were also seven or eight women who were members.

The co-op was an idea created by those who knew how to earn their bread with a pen but not with a scale. To me it was obvious from the beginning that it would fail. At the meeting my friend U. and I were strongly opposed to it. It was childish to think that a business could be set up in such a simple way. Suzuki's face became red with anger. He said to us, "You guys are against everything. Do you want to let the union go bankrupt?"

My idea was this. We may choose one store and decide that the union members will buy only from that store. We will get a percentage of the profits and give a part of it to the customers and the rest to the union. This way we don't need any capital and are guaranteed to make money. A few officers began to see my point, but those who had been convinced from the beginning by their 'god' Suzuki's proposal for a co-op rejected my idea. They were very optimistic about their money-making scheme.

Not even half a year had passed before they began to say the co-op was short of money. They discussed it at a board meeting but nobody was ready to offer money to save it. Vegetables and fruit remained in the store windows for days where they slowly spoiled. The people from the Minshu would come to the store to get money for paper and ink and they would even come to collect their salary. Sometimes they took merchandise in place of their salary. There was a rumour that one union executive with many children was getting things free of charge from the store. It was said that the union was feeding those kids. This sounded quite believable to me.

As I had predicted, the board finally decided that they couldn't continue and would give the store to a Mr. I. Again my friend U. and I were opposed to this idea. Members at the board meeting do not have the right to decide to give the store away. The store belongs to all the shareholders. Without the consent of these people how could we give it away. I had already contended in meetings that a team should be elected to investigate the accounts. We insisted. "Remember that honest members passionately supported the store and invested their money. How can we let them lose their money. Investigate thoroughly and collect the money from those who owe, make them pay it back. The Labour Union and the co-op are two separate things. Their accounting must be separate too," I told them.

As I persisted a quarrel began. Those who were conscious of their guilt urged that a vote be taken. "I won't let you vote," I insisted, "it wouldn't be valid. Did you guys mean to cheat honest members from the beginning?" Suzuki became furious. He proposed the motion that U. and I be kicked out of the union. It was passed. The pretext for our expulsion was that we were communist elements disturbing the order of the union. However they explained it, I think they were rightly afraid. Their position would be threatened by our presence.

My friend U. and I left the board. From that time on Suzuki and the Youth League loathed each other like cats and dogs.

The Village Youth Association

I was also expelled from the Isoda Youth Association[12] over the issue of changing the name of the association. To change the name and improve the quality of the youth association had already been advocated by leaders such as Kondo Ichizo. After he became sick and went to Japan the issue had been set aside. Kondo used to be the representative of the Isoda Youth Association and one of the leaders of the youth association movement comprising eight groups. In his time, the youth association movement was in its heyday. Youth conferences and lectures were often organized. Four or five hundred people would gather in Orange Hall to attend a mock parliament and were greatly impressed by debates between 'members' of the ruling party and opposition. My blood still dances with excitement when I remember that time. In those days young people were enthusiastic. But they are gone, along with that time. Those who raised questions and 'attacked the government,' and those 'ministers' who responded so eloquently, are almost all dead now.

When we proposed to rename the Isoda Youth Association and began to discuss it with the supporting members of the village, some people began to spread the rumour that I was a labour unionist and that our proposal was being helped along by the communist boss, Suzuki Etsu. One day villagers led by members of an older group marched into an association meeting held at the Japanese language school. I knew that a youth association member secretly opposed to the our proposal had played the role of spy and informed the older group that no-one was really supporting me. But everyone knew that that guy had a thick head.

I explained, "The times have changed. We now have those who come from outside Isoda village as members. There are young people who feel that they cannot come into the association because of the name Isoda. There is only the Isoda association for all the Shigaken people. To be fair to those from other villages, we should change the name and invite those who are interested." Because my explanation sounded reasonable to everyone, five or six members of the older group, feeling defeated, jumped over the table to beat me up. In fact, they had been angry before this, believing that I was a communist. Figuring that they outnumbered us they began to insist on a vote. "Why a vote?," I opposed. "You guys are only supporting members of the association. There was no right to vote for non-members. I'm explaining this to you only because we want your support. We could have made a decision without approaching you but we preferred to be polite. You guys are not here to vote." As I argued against voting, other youth association members stood up and said that the older group had no right to vote.

Members of the older group said, "If you say you can't manage the association without changing the name, we're going to show you how it's done. It was a great mistake on my part to say, "Go ahead and do it if you can." Eventually the Isoda Youth Association fell into the hands of the older group, but it was obvious from the beginning that they had no will or ability to continue. I was expelled by non-members under the name of the youth association. They said that since I was responsible for dragging the association in the wrong direction; by kicking me out they could attract more people. But the association kept shrinking and finally disappeared.

So the Isoda Youth Association was crushed by the older group, but who knows, it may have been its fate to fade away with time. Other youth associations did not survive for long after that either.

Spring

I had an operation for my hemorrhoids and spent time away from work recovering. I became bored of not working so I asked the shoemaker O., a member of the youth league, to teach me shoe repairing. I had no intention of this becoming a career, it was just something to pass the time. At that time Father had gone back to Japan and I was living with my brother in the same cabin on Heatley. One night a guy five or six years older than myself with a shoe store near Powell and Main came over and begged me to buy all the tools and supplies in the store for five hundred dollars. He said he was desperate to close up. I declined, saying that I had no intention of becoming a shoe repairman. He began to come to my place almost every night. I kept on refusing. But he was so persistent. He resorted to tears to get my sympathy, begging me to save his life. I thought I was a stubborn man, but he was more stubborn. I unwillingly gave him the five hundred dollars, as if giving to a charity.

It was a big effort to move all those tools into a small room. By trying to kill time I ended up in big trouble. I felt stupid. For four or five months I just left all the things there, but then I began to wonder how I could get rid of it all. Finally I thought of opening up a store, putting these things in the store and eventually selling it all. In the meantime I thought I could work as a shoe repairman. I was still an amateur but so what. I had tools and supplies.

I opened a store at the corner of Clark and Hastings. The rent was thirty-five dollars. It was a working-class district. I thought that even if the workmanship was not very good, if I made sturdy shoes and sold them cheaply I could attract customers. Somehow I managed, making it up as I went along, and I began to improve. I bought new shoes and sold them too. The prices were very low so business was not that bad after all. I even dared to take orders for mountain shoes and managed to make at least a few pairs. My days were a struggle for survival, but there was spring in my youth.

After being expelled from the labour union, my friend U. and I edited a monthly pamphlet, Seido, the organ of the proletarian Youth League. Every month we received a magazine called Taiheiyo Rodosha from San Francisco and Senki from Japan and distributed copies.[13] We met twice a month at U.'s house to study Marxist Leninism. Usually fifteen or sixteen people gathered. We were all serious. My friend U. had three children. His wife was a very nice person.

Copies of the newspaper and magazine were divided up for each member to distribute. One night after work I went to U.'s place to pick up my share. There was a girl there that I had never seen before. I asked Mrs. U. who she was. She said the girl was the daughter of an acquaintance, visiting from Japan for the summer vacation. For a while after that I did not see her since I was always in a hurry and did not have time to visit the house. But later, when I went to a store in the neighbourhood for a delivery, I ran into the girl and Mrs. U. shopping. For the first time I saw the girl's face clearly. I thought she was fourteen or fifteen years old. She was slender and tall. Without make-up her skin was so white it seemed as if she was half white. She had a pretty face.

Later when I stopped by at their place, Mrs. U. said to the girl, "Yoshiko, ask Mr. Takahashi." And then to me, "She has a lot of time on her hands so she wants to borrow some good books from you . . ."

According to Mrs. U., Yoshiko was visiting Canada to live with her father for the first time. Her father lived in an apartment in the neighbourhood, but he worked on the boats and was only home on Saturday night. That's why she was virtually living with the U. family. After summer vacation Yoshiko wanted to go back to Japan to live with her grandparents. She wanted to enter a women's University and hoped to become a doctor. But her father did not want to let her leave.

The summer vacation ended and neither the father nor the daughter wished to leave one another, so they decided she would stay for one year. In the meantime I heard that she had started to attend fourth grade at Strathcona Public School to learn English.

As I lent her some books we began to talk. I told her that I had a shoe repair store in the neighbourhood and that she could visit me in her free time. Soon she began to come to my store after she finished school at three o'clock. She told me later that at first she was too shy to enter the store and just passed by several times. She started to visit me once or twice a week and sometimes stayed until closing time. A few times I invited her to have supper with me at a Chinese restaurant. I would walk her to her house and then go to meetings and attend to other business. She invited me to come for supper at her place. First I declined, telling her not to bother with that. But she insisted. She asked me for an evening free of meetings. So one day she came to my store to meet me just before closing time. We started to have supper regularly after that, but I tried not to stay too late. I didn't think it was a good thing to drag a young woman around or to stay at her house late when she was alone.

Yoshiko asked me to take her to a Youth League meeting. First I used a pseudonym for her. But then when Yoshiko's father started to come to these meetings he asked me to use her real name. So after that she was known by her real name. I introduced myself to her father and explained how we had become friends. I wanted him to understand that I was not trying to sneak into his house like a thief while he was away. "She is lonely, so please be a good friend to her," he said. He knew that I was not a punk but had a job and was working hard. He said, "A young man like you is always welcome. Please come visit her without *enryo*."[14] This was nice, but I was too busy anyways and I was not so naive as to be flattered by his offer.

We gradually became aware that the distance between us was getting smaller and smaller. One day Yoshiko told me about her experience in a girl's high school dormitory. "At ten o'clock every night the supervisor would come around. She said goodnight and turned off the lights. Everybody responded by saying goodnight in unison. As her footsteps faded away the whispering began. The seniors would talk without *enryo* about boys. The rest of us listened attentively. As I listened to them I began to dream about the time when I would fall in love." Yoshiko added, in a quiet voice, "I think the time has come." She took my hand. I guess she was putting into practice what she had learned from her high school seniors. We were excited . . .

In the beginning we didn't think about marriage. I vaguely thought that the relationship might one day result in marriage, but we never talked about it and made no promises. Although I was already twenty-six, I felt I was far from ready to get married, but Yoshiko became impatient. She was intelligent and independent for her age, but she seemed to me still too young. I said, "Let's wait at least two years." She had a strong longing to have a happy family because she was an only child, had lost her mother and had been separated from her father. But I thought it was not sufficient reason for marriage. I also thought that we had to get to know more about each other. "Why do we have to wait two years? Why not now?," she protested. Her face as it was at that moment still comes back to me today.

She wanted to get married partly for the sake of her father. She knew that her father was alone in this country without relatives and that the best way to make him happy would be for her to get married and have children. In fact, he used to say that he was looking forward to nothing more than seeing his own grandchildren. No matter what their situation was, I could not change what I had once decided. Many times I explained to Yoshiko, "I'm not ready. You're only seventeen years old. Let's wait." I don't know whether she could not trust me or was disappointed with me. She finally went back to Japan.

I had almost decided to talk to her father, but then I thought that since we were not officially engaged, to talk to him would not be appropriate. Later I heard that he mentioned to someone else that Yoshiko would not have had to go back to Japan if Takahashi had agreed to marry her. It was also later that I got to know something else. Yoshiko had decided to come visit Canada again and was waiting to take a boat from her island to the Japanese mainland. The ocean was too rough and the sailings were cancelled. While waiting for the weather to improve, she had received a telegram notifying her that her father in Canada had died suddenly from liver cancer. She gave up the trip.

I didn't know anything about her father's illness and death. By that time I was busy working at my fruit and vegetable store on Robson. He had been a good man. To this man who had been so trusting and understanding towards me, I could not even give words of consolation and farewell. I regret it deeply still.

After a while I received a letter from Yoshiko expressing her wish to come back to Canada. Many things were in that letter. I wrote a polite letter of condolence apologizing that I had not visited her father during his illness nor attended his funeral. I suppose my letter was not what she had expected. Or there may have been some other reason. I never received a letter from her again.

Depression Years

After a while the Great Depression hit. Unemployed people began to overflow into the streets and every day there were workers' rallies and demonstrations demanding jobs and food. In those days there was no unemployment insurance, no pension, no welfare. So when a worker lost his job, he found himself broke and unable to cope with even the next day. Workers went to City Hall and demanded relief. The government began to issue food stamps.

Many Japanese also lost their jobs. Since the Japanese Labour Union did nothing, Youth League members began to visit the homes of the unemployed workers and urged them to ask for relief. Japanese had a tendency to feel ashamed to ask for and receive help from the government. Many preferred to implore friends and relatives to lend them money rather than receive relief. White people organized themselves, under the guidance of the Communist Party, into the Unemployed Worker's Union throughout Canada. They issued pamphlets appealing for workers to receive government relief and pressured the government to introduce unemployment insurance. They sent leaders to the provincial and federal governments. Representing Asian workers, I went to British Columbia's capital, Victoria, along with five white delegates. Twenty-seven representatives entered the parliament. I read a short plea along with two white persons. Outside the parliament thousands of unemployed workers were rallying.

Matsui and a white man went to Ottawa as representatives for British Columbia. Delegates from all over Canada were demanding unemployment insurance from the Ottawa government. It was a cold February. We didn't have money for train fare so they had to hitch a ride on a freight train. When they returned from Ottawa and reported to the rally that the CPR engineer had appreciated their cause and invited them into a warm engine room, the crowd responded with great applause and we sang the "Internationale." Today Canada's unemployment insurance system exists thanks to such movements and the efforts of our predecessors many years ago.

In Vancouver there were many meetings and rallies for unemployed workers. One night I made a speech at the Powell Grounds. I urged other Japanese not to hesitate. "Go ahead and get relief without *enryo*," I told them.

I don't know if the Japanese really felt ashamed to take relief from the government or whether they felt shy to be seen receiving it because it was supposed to be shameful. There was a man who claimed that it degraded not only the individual who asked the government to feed him, but every Japanese. That was Morii of the Showa Club.[15] He would argue that the Japanese should collect donations among themselves and help those unemployed and those in trouble. According to him, it was *yamato-damashii*[16] to refuse to be dependent on the government even in a time of great hardship. I countered. "It would not be a shame. Go without *enryo*. It would be more shameful to cause trouble for your family, employer and friends by borrowing money and not being able to pay them back. And you would have to lower yourself by begging from them," I insisted.

One day when I was walking down Powell Street, five or six men from the Showa Club attacked me. They knocked me down, kicking me. For five minutes they continued to beat me up, shouting, "You filthy son of a bitch! You're a disgrace to the community! You deserve to die!" Then they were gone. I found myself surrounded by a crowd of curious people. Ignorance has a terrible power.

There was a man who received unemployment relief. An acquaintance began to talk about this man behind his back. He mocked him as if he had been begging on the street. Times have changed. The same man who was critical is now receiving supplementary pension from the government by hiding the money he has.

I offered the back of my store for the unemployed worker's union to use for typing up their pamphlets. Once the manuscript was typed, Y. took it to the attic of my aunt's house and printed the pamphlets. Then we would give them to a certain white girl, meeting her each time in a different place. I was the one who bought the paper from a Japanese salesman. The man, T., was from the same village I came from. I told him, "Never say anything to anybody." The pamphlets were not supposed to be sold but actually we charged two cents for the cost of the paper. I was the treasurer. The police and their spies searched everywhere for the secret print shop but I guess they were not imaginative enough to think of the Japanese.

Both Feet on the Ground

As I learned about socialism, those who had seemed to be so great and admirable stopped being great and admirable. I began to see their selfishness and hypocrisy. Once I had been timid and shy in public but now I was not afraid to speak out about my beliefs. Quite a few times I made speeches at Orange Hall to several hundred people. I also developed the ability to write for newspapers and magazines, which had been unthinkable for a person like myself without education.

Socialism gave me a strong confidence. Before I had been standing on my hands, seeing society upside-down. I had been educated to view things that way. But now both my feet are firmly on the ground. Socialism revolutionized me.

One who believes in socialism has to be responsible for his actions. Even if he says and writes fine things, if his behaviour is not right people won't trust him. Thus he will be hurting socialism in its true sense. Socialists must be trustworthy.

I worked hard. I told myself not to cause trouble for other people. Well, it is true that I was kicked out twice and had some heated arguments, but that was something different.

I decided to carry out my longtime plan of buying some land and building a house on it. The land that I bought in a suburb of Vancouver was located on high ground. The air was good and it was quiet. Behind my lot there was a large tract of land reserved for a park. From higher up on the hill the city of Vancouver could be seen down below. In those days a lot was only fifty dollars. There was no water system and no road. Today fine houses stand there and I hear real estate prices are pretty high. Simon Fraser University was also built nearby.

Father had come back from Japan. After an operation for hemorrhoids he was recovering at home. Every Sunday my brother and I would go out with a packed lunch and father would ask where we were going. But we didn't tell him the truth, we made small talk, evading the question. If I had said something about buying the land and building a house he would have opposed us. So I told my brother to keep quiet about it.

But I could not keep the secret forever. One day I finally told him that we were clearing the land. As I expected, he got upset. He said that it was senseless to build a house while he was sick. "Are you planning to spend the rest of your life in this country? We don't have anything in Japan but that lousy shack and you want to build a house in this country! What's gotten in to you? How foolish of you!," he shouted.

"It was primarily for you, Papa, that we decided to build a house," I told my father. "If you keep on drinking every day in this tiny semi-basement cabin with bad air and no place for even planting flowers, you'll shorten your life.

"Papa, you haven't been working a day since Hastings mill closed down. If you stay home I'd like you to stay in a nice place with more space and better air. I'm not even asking you to find some money for me . . ." Father insisted, "Our house in Japan is not luxurious but it is still our house. Why do you have to build a new house here?" I explained, "I know our villagers are doing the opposite thing. While building big houses in Japan where nobody lives, they are staying in small, rented apartments for a long time in this country. I won't do such a stupid thing." Father spat out, "I won't go live in your place. I won't help you either."

We laid the cement foundations and then began to build the house. But Father did not come to help, although some friends helped us. But finally Father, who had been so vehemently opposed, began to come to the house when it was almost finished. When we moved to the new house he came with us, with a happy face, as if he had always been looking forward to this.

For a while Father complained that he was lonely and would often go out to the city. But later he must have become accustomed to the new environment. He began to chop firewood, till the soil, cultivate vegetables and flowers and keep chickens. Thus he slowly learned to become a country man again. Finally he became so used to it that when he went to Vancouver he would return early, as if fleeing the city. I asked him, "Why don't you spend more time playing?" "I feel more relaxed at home," was his answer.

By that time he had stopped getting drunk and going to the Chinese gambling parlours. Now that he had changed, I felt sorry and wanted to offer him a drink.

Sometimes on my way back from work I bought some Japanese *sake* to bring home for Father. He would drink a bottle of four *go*[17] and save some for later. After pouring to fill the glass halfway he would examine it and say, "A little more." Then he picked up the bottle and examined the amount that remained. I was watching his eyes. He was just like a child told to eat only half of the chocolates. He loved *sake* so much.

Even when I arrived home late at night I would wake my father and show him what I had bought. He was happy and all smiles. The same *sake* used to make me cry, but now offering it to my father became one of my pleasures.

The pain of my hemorrhoids did not go away. I sold the shoe store and was recuperating at home. Father clung to the hope that he would see me with a bride and be able to return to Japan with a relieved mind. But I tried to persuade him not to worry about me and go home to join Mother. I had saved up ten thousand yen in the Japanese bank by that time; the goal which I had been working towards all these years. With that money my parents' retirement would be secure.

At last the time of father's departure came. That morning he said to me, "I have no worries about you, but I worry about your kid brother. Please stand by him." His eyes were wet. I wished to separate on good terms with him. I had cooked *sekihan*[18]. Father entrusted me with my brother, with whom he had so many fights when he was drunk. Father was now worrying about this unworthy son. I was touched by his deep, fatherly affection. I cried. I didn't know that I would never see him again.

Departure and arrival

In the spring of 1934 I bought a fruit and vegetable store on Robson for six hundred dollars. I knew that its real value was less than half of that, but the middle man asked me to buy without trying to lower the price because the owners were in serious financial trouble. So I accepted it without a fuss. I remodelled the store and stocked it with fresh produce. I needed some capital so I asked Mr. O. to do me a great favour and lend me five hundred dollars. He was a cousin of my mother and a very generous man. I never forget that without the direct and indirect help of these people I would not be here today. The small store became busy and five people began to work for me.

On Saturdays I went to the farmer's market in New Westminster. Both white and Japanese farmers gathered there to sell their produce. There were seven or eight Japanese farmers from Sun Valley, Surrey, Strawberry Hill and Queensboro selling vegetables and fruit. Ever since the Manchurian Incident [1931 Japanese invasion of Manchuria] Chinese merchants were boycotting Japanese farmers, so they were having a hard time. Every Japanese farmer begged me to buy from him. I started to go out to their farms twice a week. First my partner E. came with me but then he made up all sorts of excuses and stopped coming. But I continued. As we began to sell large quantities I began to go every evening. It wasn't easy to do it after a day's work at the store. I would come back with a full truckload. We sold not only at our store, but also to other Japanese vegetable stores at the city market the next morning. I would have to go to the city market at five o'clock in the morning. My body became as worn-out as a limp rag. I was young, but working from five o'clock in the morning to midnight every day was a bit too much.

I was married in February 1935 to the daughter of my Japanese farmer acquaintance. The following year my younger brother got married to my wife's younger sister. First my wife's family told me to choose either the older or younger daughter. But after all, between my brother and I, we got both. You can imagine how happy my parents in Japan were. I had earlier promised them that I would return to Japan with my bride so they could meet her and their grandchildren. So they had been longing for that day to come. Father had spent over three years in bed after suffering a stroke, but by that time (1936) he became well enough to walk with a cane. The doctor is said to have warned him never to drink *sake* again; drinking would be fatal. When he organized the memorial service commemorating the fifty years since his older brother's death, father offered *sake* to his guests. He had a sudden desire to drink with them and would not listen to those who tried to stop him. It is said that he was feeling ready to die now that the memorial service was accomplished. As the doctor had predicted, father died at the end of April.

My son was born in early May. Father died without being able to wait for just a few weeks. He loved *sake* so much.

When I received the news of father's death I was disheartened. I didn't expect to feel so sad. It felt unreal. I still remember that I had to run to the bathroom to hide because I couldn't stop the tears from flowing.

Visiting Home

At the end of 1936, as I had promised mother, we left for Japan. We celebrated the New Year on the boat and arrived in Yokohama on the seventh of January. We were accompanied by my wife's mother.

At the Yokohama port the seaway police stopped me and told me to come with them. They took me to a small room where there were two people. "What are you doing in Canada?," they asked. "I have a little business." "So you're doing okay financially. What kind of organizations do you belong to?" "For my business I'm a member of a co-operative." "What is the purpose of your visit?" "To show my wife and child to my parents." "You may go," the officer said politely.

I arrived in my cherished native village where I had been born and grown up. As we stood in front of the house I said to my wife, "Isn't it an imposing house?" Everyone laughed. Mother was inside. She was so excited she didn't know what to do with herself. She moved around nervously, sniffling and wiping her tears on the sleeve of her kimono.

For this special occasion she had lighted candles in the family altar. Mother might have thought that my late father would be watching our homecoming. We three sat before the altar and said, as if to a living person, "Thanks to you, we are home." As we mumbled namuamidabutsu[19] we placed our hands together and bowed.

You may find it contradictory for an atheist like myself to chant namuamidabutsu at the altar. I don't see it that way. This phrase has taken care of the passing of all our ancestors. To express our gratitude to our ancestors there is no other phrase and no other place.

I embraced mother. "I'm back." As my lips brushed her cheek I felt her tears. I was crying and all around the others were crying. Pointing to my wife holding our baby, I said, "This is the bride." Mother said, "I can't see her face through my tears." When my mother gently ruffled her grandson's hair he began to cry loudly. I guess my mother's crying face made him afraid. He was only seven months old. In my life this is the only time I cried tears of joy.

The next day mother said, "I'm happy that you're back, but it's so sad to think that you'll leave again." I said, "You are already thinking of us leaving? We have just arrived!"
Crying, she said, "I can't stand the thought that such a sweet baby will be gone soon." I guess when one reaches old age one becomes emotional, crying at the slightest things, happy or sad.

A few days later a policeman from the village came with a warning from regional headquarters. He told me to inform them if I intended to travel beyond one mile from the village. Neither my wife nor my mother knew what this meant so they didn't worry. I answered simply that I understood, but later ignored the warning. The policeman never returned. At that time I was still a member of the Communist Party of Canada. So I could have been punished under Japan's Law for Maintenance of the Public Peace.

After some time, mother's younger brother, Uncle S., came and advised me with much hesitation, "I hear that you are a socialist. It's not a good thing." "Uncle," I answered, "socialists try to improve everyone's life and build a world in which people help each other and starving people no longer have to worry about their next meal. I believe this is socialism. I wonder why you think this is not good."
"I guess the socialism you believe in is different," he said. I think he immediately felt my sincerity.

While I was busy working in Canada, I had always been concerned about my family in Japan. The first thing was the health of my parents. Father had been in bad shape after having a stroke and mother had been losing her strength to asthma. I had also been worried about mother's family.

One day mother said to me, "All the money you earned with the sweat of your labour and sent to me is being wasted by my brothers. It's pitiful that I have such poor brothers."

"You shouldn't say that," I told her, "We should be happier to help others than to be helped. I feel that my hard work was worth something after all." Mother said repeatedly, "Good things will happen to you. The more you please others the more good things will come to you."

My mother's family was about to collapse into bankruptcy. Uncle I. was so old that pressuring him was like whipping a dying horse. It seemed that only in his son H. could any hope be placed. I had already felt, while in Canada, that it would become necessary to bring H. back to Canada with us. So I had made all the necessary preparations before leaving for Japan.[20] I told only mother about my intentions. I said to her, "Don't tell anybody. I might decide to go back to Canada without using H.'s passport."

When we had arrived in Japan H. had just returned to the village from two years of military service. Flattered by all the attention and admiration he received from the villagers, he became conceited, thinking he was a superior person. He refused to take up regular work. On calm, windless days he would dig up clams from the lake to make extra money and bicycle into the town of Hikone to sit in a cafe.

H. was avoiding our house, and I knew the reason. Like myself, he had grown up with the ideology of chukun-aikoku[21]. In elementary school he had been made to salute the emperor's portrait every morning, and when he was a naive young man he was taken and brainwashed with the propaganda of yamato-damashii — the power of the Japanese spirit. He came back to the village believing it would be an honour to offer his body as a weapon. It was all too natural for him not to want to visit a house tainted with socialism. He must have thought it very shameful to have a traitor to the country in the family. In my opinion he was the problem in the family. One night Uncle S. was at our place for a bath. Mother was tending the fire, talking with Uncle as he sat in the bath. Sitting on the hearth reading a newspaper I overheard their conversation. Uncle S. said, "I have given up and will leave the village and go to Osaka to become a beggar there. As you know H. is fooling around every day without contributing a penny. The interest on the money that we borrowed from the cooperative is increasing and soon our house will be taken. There is no way that I can stay in the village."

I wondered how H. could be so insensitive and stupid, when his own house was in such dire straits and his own father about to leave to become a beggar. Having become accustomed to not working, he had become conceited and was now saying that he would volunteer to become a military policeman. Once the house is taken and there is no place for him to sleep and eat, would the emperor and the government feed him?

One evening, at my request, mother invited H. for supper. As we chatted I tried to determine his feelings and thoughts about his future, but I couldn't discover anything particularly interesting. Finally I asked him if he wanted to go to Canada. He said, bluntly, "I want to but I can't."

I gave him a lecture. "You are wrong if you think that Canada is a place where you can play around and earn money to feed yourself. You are now without a regular job, fooling around on your bicycle. In Canada such a man would be no good. But if you promise to listen to what I say and work hard, I have the means to take you to Canada with me." At this moment H.'s eyes widened and came to life, my mother said later. "However, if I decide that I should not take you . . ."

"Please take me! I will obey you and work hard. Please . . ." He looked pale. Mother interjected. "H., listen well to your older cousin who cares about you so much. You are so lucky," she said. So H. who had avoided our house began to visit often after he found out that he could go to Canada.

Gathering Clouds

In Japan it is already mild spring weather in March. To kill time I began to go fishing. One morning I dug up earthworms and put them in an empty can. Later I discovered that the can had disappeared. I looked around but couldn't find it. Mother said that a neighbour's boy was playing around there and probably took it.

Mother wanted me to fix the fence in front of the house. I went to the store to buy nails but there were none left. When I was fishing I saw people scooping old rusting metal from the water with a hoe at the end of a bamboo pole. They collected the metal scraps in sacks. This is no joke, I thought, they must be preparing for a war. Next door there was a fifteen-year-old boy, an only son. I told him, "By the time you have to go for military service Japan might be at war. Even if you have to be put in jail, never go to war." Well, this was certainly communist propaganda. If I had said something like this in a public place I would have been the one to be put in jail.

Nowadays it is no big deal to say that I'm against the war. Nobody

Neighbourhood children in front of the house in 1990 that Genshichi Takahashi built himself in Burnaby, British Columbia. "The house was seized and sold dirt cheap."

Photo by Keibo Oiwa

would think it is communist propaganda or that I am a traitor to the country. Even the patriots who opposed the war for the sake of the country and the lives of compatriots were accused of being traitors, jailed, and even killed. Even those who remained silent were seen as opponents of the war efforts. Those scholars, intellectuals, politicians and religious leaders who had pronounced 'great' thoughts were now dancing in the hands of the military.

My apprehension became justified much sooner than I thought. In the fall of 1937, following our return to Canada, the Japanese military instigated the Shanghai Incident and invaded China. As I had feared, the boy next door was recruited as a soldier and sent to the South Seas where he was left stranded without weapons or food and died like an animal. His father was dead but his elderly mother was praying to the gods for his return. She never knew where and when he died. She never received his ashes. The only thing she received was a telegram notifying her that her son had earned the honour of dying in battle.

Wanting to stay as many days as possible with Mother I extended my stay from May to June. Mother had coughing fits at night. I woke and caressed her back. Her undershirt was soaking wet with sweat and I helped her change. Seeing such things, it was hard to think of returning to Canada. I felt as if my feet were bound by heavy chains. Although I knew I was being an irresponsible son, I had to leave Japan where I had no means to make a living. I promised mother that my brother's family would visit her in the fall. In the end they visited one year later, in October 1939. By that time they had two sons which made Mother very happy.

I told my sister-in-law not to hurry back to Canada but to stay in Japan as long as possible and take good care of Mother. One day in February of the following year I received a telegram notifying me of Mother's death. My sadness was less intolerable than of the time of Father's death. I wonder if that was because I had seen her suffer from asthma. I told myself that after knowing that her two sons had formed their own families and seeing the faces of her grandchildren, Mother did not have any regrets and must have felt her life was fulfilled. The thought that my brother and his wife were able to be with her when she was on her deathbed and helped her pass away peacefully, may have consoled me.

My brother's family came back to Canada after taking care of things in Japan. The boat that they took was the last to cross the Pacific. If they had missed it they would have been stranded in Japan during those long days of the war. Perhaps my brother would have been sent to the war front.

Big Black Scar

After returning from Japan I began a wholesale business in the Powell Street store. There were five associates but only three of us put down initial capital. My friend E. was the nominal president but he would come as late as nine in the morning and spend time talking about the war. After lunch he would take money from the cash register and go to the horse races. Only I and another young man would work from the morning until late at night. It was obvious that such a business would not work. For the first ten months I worked without receiving a cent of salary. From anybody's point of view I was a hopeless idiot. Finally I quit. My loss was nine hundred dollars. This was a very expensive price to pay. But for that price I got the conviction that this business could work if done right.

The next year I opened a wholesale business on Georgia Street. My capital was five hundred dollars that I borrowed from the *tanomoshi*.[22] A used two-ton truck cost three hundred and fifty dollars. The scale was ten dollars at the second hand shop on Main Street. Rent was thirty-five dollars, printing ten dollars, telephone three dollars, etcetera. The five hundred dollars was gone.

This was the capital for the wholesale business. I know it is hard to believe. Even I couldn't believe it. But it is true. I continued with these reckless ways. I was still young. Thanks to the poverty that I grew up with I had a strong instinct for survival and wasn't afraid to take risks.

After awhile I began to deal in rhubarb, asparagus, strawberries and so on. I did business with the good farmers with good products. In order to earn their trust it was best to pay them regularly and without delay. Each day I would pay them for the products I had taken the day before. But as my customers would not give me cash for the goods I sold, I always had a hard time finding the cash to pay the farmers. I had to ask for a lot of help from my wife's parents. It was all thanks to them that I was able to continue. I worked very, very hard. There was no time to rest. This hardworking body was my only asset. The business began to go well. The following year I had five people working for me.

Financial hardships did not stop tormenting me. The more business I did the more unpaid credit accumulated. Although on the books I had a fair profit, I was always short of money. Japanese merchants would not pay me (even while paying the other wholesalers). But I could not tell them that I would stop selling to them unless they paid. For example, a friend of mine, K., always owed me at least one thousand dollars. When it went beyond one thousand dollars I would tell him, "Hey man, it's over one thousand, pay some of it." He was in financial trouble and I wanted to help him but I was in trouble too.

In the wintertime there were no local vegetables so I had to go to Seattle to import vegetables and fruit. I think I was the first Japanese to do this. I went once a week, sometimes twice. I would load six to seven tons in my two ton truck. My driver and I would leave at two o'clock in the morning and arrive in Seattle around six o'clock. We bought here and there, asked union members to pack up the produce and tried to leave the city by three o'clock so we could make it to the border. (At four o'clock the commercial customs office would be closed). There was no time to even have a cup of coffee. At the border we would have to unload the stuff into a customs hut. After getting the go ahead from the officers my driver and I would reload it all into the truck. We rarely had it all unloaded back at the store before eleven o'clock. I would finally eat something worthy of being called a meal at around midnight. My body was completely drained.

I worked myself to the bone and finally established the foundation of a business and then the Pacific War broke out and I was forcibly sent to road camp. The house was seized and sold dirt cheap and there was no way I could save my business.

The government promised us that until the end of the war the Custodians would take care of our properties. We trusted the words of the government and left all our belongings behind. These were all very important things to us. They then confiscated and sold for next-to-nothing, our farmland, fishing boats, and cars, by means of the unjust law called the War Measures Act. From the beginning the government intended to deceive us.

No excuses can justify those discriminatory actions which singled out the Japanese. How could Canada portray itself to the rest of the world as a civilized, free, Christian country? There is on the face of Canada a big black scar.

What connection was there between my house and the war? They took away our legitimate livelihood, forced us to move, disposed of our properties, saying "once Japanese always Japanese." Their war was against Japan, not against Japanese Canadians. To me this simply meant that they were using the war as a pretext to persecute a coloured people. If they really meant to apply the War Measures Act to the peoples whose countries of origin were against the Allies, then they would have had to treat Italians and Germans in the same way as the Japanese. What was the difference? Why the Japanese but not the Italians and Germans? (Just be honest and say the colour of the skin was different.) Why did they perpetrate this injustice on Japanese Canadians including those born in Canada? They must explain to us in such a manner that we would be able to understand.

Canada said it was fighting fascism in order to protect freedom. But it should first fight against its own fascism. I wonder what the essential difference was between Canada's white supremacist attitude and Hitler's policy against the Jews?

Alberta Years

The three years I spent in Alberta were very hard but now I am filled with nostalgia for that time.

When we arrived in Glenwood it was already getting dark. The villagers were gathered in anticipation of our arrival. Having heard and read so much about us they were curious to see what we looked like. Someone in the crowd exclaimed in disappointment, "They just look Chinese." Before long they all went home.

I began to work as a farmhand earning fifteen cents an hour, working twelve hour days, seven days a week which came to fifty bucks a month. I would get up at six o'clock and milk fifteen cows, all before breakfast. I didn't do it very well at the very beginning, but after a week or so I began to manage. In those days there was no milking machines so that it all had to be done by hand. I would come back for a quick breakfast and then go back to take care of the pigs and cattle. I also worked in the fields. I would milk again in the evening and my day would be finished around seven o'clock.

The first winter was especially harsh. The temperature dropped to fifty below and when the notorious Alberta winds blew, it was even colder. Often when riding in from the fields with a wagon load of hay, my eyelashes would be covered with ice.

I never even had a day of rest. The work I found the hardest was digging the sugar beets and loading them onto the wagon. The next morning I couldn't get myself out of bed. The landlord came to find me and I had to really force myself to go with him. I thought I was a man of endurance but that time I almost wanted to give up. At such times I could only tell myself that I wouldn't have been in a place like this if there had been no war. As the old saying goes, "Life has it's ups and downs." I was right at the bottom of my life. I tried to encourage myself to climb my way up as fast as I could.

I worked until April of the following year. Then I asked the landlord if I could lease land from him. He asked me, "What do you intend to grow?" "Vegetables," I said. "Carrots, cabbage, and potatoes." My idea was that although this was a beet farm a large portion of the land had been set aside as fallow, this could be a good place for vegetables. The landlord then said to me, "Even if you managed to grow vegetables, there is no way that you could sell them." "If I can't sell them, I'll give them to you for your cattle and pigs," I insisted. I asked how much I could lease the land for and he told me it would be $250. Two hundred and fifty dollars! With that much money I could buy the land. For less rent I suggested paying him a percentage of my sales but he wouldn't go below two hundred and fifty. However, I wouldn't have to pay rent for the house, I'd get free manure, and I could use his farm machinery and drink milk for free.

I used his beet-sowing machine for sowing carrot seeds. I used two acres for cabbage, one and a half acres for potatoes and I also planted beets, radishes, and other vegetables. When the carrots sprouted a couple of inches, I asked my Indian friends, who lived nearby, to bring about ten women to help me do some weeding. My friend worked as a foreman and they were very happy to come to my place and earn some cash even though it wasn't very much.

My landlord did not believe me when I said I would grow vegetables but I had my own ideas. I did not waste my experience as a wholesaler in Vancouver. Other Japanese were only thinking about beets. If my neighbour had ten acres of beets, I would plant fifteen acres. We were all involved in that kind of competition. To grow ten acres of beets is unbelievably hard work. The income for that would be $350, which was not enough for a family to live on, even in the countryside. Those who had money saved were fine. But others had to borrow money from

Working in a sugar beet field, southern Alberta.

Courtesy of Japanese Canadian Cultural Centre

Genshichi and Mika Takahashi with their son Ken
in Montreal in 1946, one year after they left Alberta.

Courtesy of Mr. & Mrs. Takahashi

the landlords or ask for relief from the Commission.

I had heard that there was a POW camp for Germans near Lethbridge. I reasoned that the government would have to feed them. Instead of importing expensive vegetables in winter, they would prefer to feed them less expensive vegetables. Also I was aware that wartime regulations controlled the prices of domestically grown vegetables. There was a ceiling price of fifty dollars a ton for carrots and cabbages. In summertime the price would be low but in winter time it would be high. That is the reason why, with the landlord's agreement, I planned to make an underground food cellar. With the help of the Indians and their horses, we dug some holes, 16 by 10 feet and ten feet deep. We built in a wood structure with a roof, covered it with straw mats and earth. This variation on a root cellar would allow the vegetables to stay unfrozen in the winter time. After harvesting and putting the vegetables into the cellar I had nothing else to do but to wait. Earlier in the summer I had already asked a wholesaler in Lethbridge to let me know when the price reached its ceiling. When it got pretty cold the orders came to send out five tons each of carrots and cabbage. I hired a person who regularly went to Lethbridge from the village to buy coal, to transport my vegetables. Loading the vegetables in bags and then onto the truck was all done by the Indians. Usually they didn't have work so they were very happy to receive fifty cents an hour. While loading the stuff onto the truck the landlord came out to see me. "How much are you selling this for?," he asked. "Fifty dollars a ton," I said. He was shocked. "Is this all you have?" I told him that I had three more loads like this to go. I'm sure he regretted that he didn't go in with me for a percentage.

The following year around Raymond, the relocated Japanese beet farmers rushed to grow vegetables. Although they weren't doing it on as large a scale as me, I think they heard about my success. It is understandable that they would want to change from back-breaking work where they only earned $350 a year to something easier and more profitable. What they did not understand was that to sell the product is much more difficult than to grow it. In fact I heard that many people had to let their vegetable crops rot without even harvesting them because of a lack of a market. Since I anticipated the farmers would follow my lead, I tried to grow different crops during the summer. Using my Lethbridge connection I sent lettuce, cucumbers and cauliflower which was all bought up. I reduced the amount of vegetables I stored in the cellar and fortunately I sold everything at the top ceiling price.

Before I left Alberta I went to Lethbridge to thank my wholesaler and the guy said, "Thank you for supplying me with vegetables when I needed them. Were you a farmer in B.C.?" "No, I was a wholesaler of fruit and vegetables like yourself." "Oh, that's why!" As he shook my hand, he wished me good luck. In my wholesale days I was taken advantage of and I also made many mistakes which, at the time, I thought was a very expensive tuition. But now I know that it was time and money well spent.

I don't want to sound like I'm bragging but I think, among the Japanese who were sent to farm sugar beets during the war, I was the first to grow vegetables. I don't think I would have done it if there hadn't been a POW camp near Lethbridge. To be honest I was violating the law. Under the War Measures Act we enemy aliens were not allowed to buy land nor lease it. The landlord was not aware of that.

My business ideas weren't always winners. When I was still working as a farmhand, my Japanese friend Mr. M. who lived nearby, urged me to raise pigs. I told him that I had no time and I had no experience raising pigs. But he assured me that he would help so we bought two young pigs from the landlord.

The pigs grew fast. We castrated the male pig, fattened him up and sold him. The female had six little piglets and soon we had more than thirty pigs. To feed them all was an immense task. We bought a truck load of pig feed from the landlord. We had to mulch it all up with a machine hoping that by the time they had eaten it all we would make some money and be able to afford some more. But the baby pigs, although they ate a lot, didn't grow. Something was wrong. One day Mr. M.'s son came to tell me that one of the pigs had died. The next morning two more died. The pigs were all in one corner of the pig pen, eyes closed and shivering. I had to call a neighbouring farmer who knew about pigs to come and see. He told us that they weren't good anymore and that we had to kill them all. He also thought that this was because the stud-pig was ill. He asked us which one we used. When I told him where we got the stud, he told us that the same thing had happened to somebody else. Our plan to make a couple of hundred dollars each was a total disaster. At least we saved three of them and then killed them to eat. They were very tasty. The best pork is from castrated pigs weighing about a hundred and seventy-five pounds. I lost around a hundred dollars on this venture.

There was a highway in front of my house which I travelled to go to

Ken Takahashi in Glenwood, southern Alberta, with Mr. Statz,
a Mormon farmer who became good friends with the Takahashi family.

Courtest of Mr. & Mrs. Takahashi

Mr. & Mrs. Takahashi at home in Montreal, autumn 1989.

Photo by Eddie Hillel

the village store or the nearby town. Almost every day Indians would go to the village store to shop or just to hang out. I would ride with the Indians on their wagons. The Indian reserve was on the other side of the river. This was the river where I went to fish for the large pike.

Those days we were eating pretty cheap and good meat. Most of the Indians were poor but some had large pieces of land where they grew wheat and had many cattle and horses. Since the government gave the Indians welfare money to live on many of them were living without any sort of regular job. Because the government managed the Indian lands the people couldn't sell their products on their own but had to go through a government agent. The Government would then keep all the money and only let it out in small amounts.

The Indians would come around noon and tell me, "We are going to kill a cow tonight, do you want some?" Usually they cut a cow into four. The front quarter was twenty-five cents a pound and the back quarter was thirty-five cents a pound. I always bought the back quarter. In the village there was only one food store, which was a grocery store and a restaurant. In the back of the store there were fifty meat lockers which were rented out for $1.25 a month. It was in this store that the Indians would sell their meat. We would get the store to butcher the quarters and store the meat in the lockers. This was very convenient for me. I soon learned that the best beef is red ox with a white face, and between two and two-and-a-half years old. This was the beef that we ate for three years.

I have so many things to write about our days in Alberta but I shouldn't dwell on that time. There is one person I don't want to forget. Soon after we arrived, a small old truck stopped in front of our house. A big tired looking farmer who was in his late sixties came around the side of the house and in a loud voice bellowed out; "Hello. I heard the Japanese people arrived here so I stopped by on my way to the fields. My fields are just beyond that road. I'm growing some strawberries. Whenever you have some time, just come down and eat some or take some for jam. Do you want to come along now?" We all got into the truck and went to the strawberry field. There was a small shack at the edge of the field. He said he lived in Cardston, a place thirty-five miles away and during the summer his income came from honey. His wife never came to farm. She was University-educated and had three sons and daughters who were all high school teachers. Cardston was the centre for Canadian Mormons.

His name was Mr. Statz and was of German origin. He was sympathetic to Japanese Canadians. Sometimes he would give me strawberries and tell us to take as many as we wanted. In the summer time Mr. Statz asked us to help him with his bee hives. So my wife went to help him and her job was to boil water and process the honey. Because of the war, sugar was rationed and therefore honey sold very well. She would come back with a can full of honey for us to eat. The next year he even bought one hive for us so we had more than enough honey for the whole year.

One day I accompanied Mr. Statz in his beat-up truck on his annual trip to sell his honey to the various villages—everybody was always waiting for him. The little money that he earned we spent in the village taverns drinking beer. To him this was an important social occasion which he looked forward to all year. As a Mormon he was not supposed to consume alcohol and coffee or smoke tobacco, but with me he would drink beer, smoke cigarettes and enjoy himself. He said, as if making an excuse, "Among ourselves we don't do it but outside everybody does." I did not consider this position hypocritical or as a double standard. I liked him and I knew he was a good honest man. In my house there was no beer or any alcohol so whenever he came by we served coffee. He enjoyed it. He was an optimist and he never worried about what the next day would bring. Although poor, he never dwelled on the fact and it never seemed to bother him.

Thus I had become friendly with the Indians and the villagers. I did not find any discrimination against us as enemy aliens. We became members of the community. In such a countryside there was not much political propaganda and nobody talked about the war. The only event in our village, it was completely Mormon, was a Mormon festival to which my wife and son were invited to attend. The Mormons came to Alberta many years ago to escape religious persecution.

In Alberta, I listened every day to the short wave radio which carried the news from Japan. We enemy aliens were prohibited from having radio receivers, particularly the ones which can receive the news from Japan. They were banned. I used a radio with a very tall antenna attached to it.

I once heard on a newscast the Japanese Prime Minister saying that; "We will defeat them all with bamboo spears if they try invade Japan." It was as stupid as trying to shoot airplanes down with bows and arrows. I was listening to the official war news but they never mentioned the

Japanese defeat or even Japanese soldiers being killed. Every report said that hundreds and thousands of enemy soldiers were killed and eliminated. According to them they defeated the enemy on Okinawa and the Iwo Jima islands and finally got to the point where they were talking about bamboo spears. I knew very well when they said Japanese soldiers had killed the enemy that it was the other way around and that when they claimed a victory they were actually defeated.

Since the farming business began to go well I was willing to continue for another year but I had figured out that a Japanese defeat was only a matter of time I wanted to go on to make a fresh start. We had no intention of staying in this place forever. The sooner we moved the better.

When the villagers heard that we were finally leaving for Eastern Canada they gathered to say goodbye. After only three years of friendship they treated us as warmly as village members. They prayed for our future happiness and well-being. The Indians who had helped us so much also came to bid us farewell.

Mr. Statz came early in the afternoon from Cardston and he took a picture of us as a souvenir. First a picture of everybody, then a picture of Mr. Statz and my son and finally of Mr. Statz himself. Even today these photographs are important to me. When the time came to leave, with his big rough hands, he held each of our hands. Then with his large meaty fist he wiped the tears from his eyes and said, "If there is any problem over there you must let me know." The words are still fresh in my ears.

After arriving in Montreal it was my dream to bring him to visit us but we could only afford a small room and we never had enough money. While waiting to get the money to bring him for a visit, his letters stopped. I kept on writing but there was no response from him or his family.

We left Alberta with heavy hearts. After all, a place which looked so desolate at the beginning turned out to be an unforgettable part of our lives.

NOTES

1. *Urashima-taro* is a well-known folk tale. Briefly the story goes like this: The hero, Taro, helps a turtle which is being bullied by a group of children. Later, the grateful turtle returns and takes him to a palace under the sea. After enjoying himself very much, Taro returns to his home to find that a great many years have passed.

2. *Ken* or prefecture. Regional associations organized on the basis of *ken* were called *Kenjin-kai*. They thrived in Japanese communities overseas.

3. Hoodlums.

4. These are Japanese intellectual magazines. *Yuben* means 'eloquence' and *Chuokoron* means 'mainstream public opinion.'

5. The Japanese word for communism is written with four Chinese characters, and the word revolution in two characters.

6. *Kaizo* means reconstruction and *Taiyo* means the sun.

7. Mitsuru Shinpo, *Kanada Nihonjin Imin Monogatari* (Tokyo: Tsukiji-shokan, 1986). The *Nihonjin-kai* (Japanese Association) or more formally, *Kanada Nihonjin-kai*, was organized in 1909 in Vancouver by forty-three "patrons" of Japan town. The central figure was Yamazaki, the owner of the newspaper *Tairiku-Nippo* (Continental Daily). *Nikkai*, an abbreviation of *Nihonjin-kai*, was commonly used.

8. Takaichi Umezuki, *Rodo-kumiai Junen-shi*. A booklet originally published in *Minshu*, Vancouver, 1931. The union, formerly called *Kanada Nihonjin Rodokumiai* or the Canadian Japanese Labour Union "was established July 1, 1920 following the strike co-organized by both Japanese and white workers at Swanson Bay in the spring of 1920."

9. Miyoko Kudo and Susan Phillips, *Vancouver no Ai: Tamura Toshiko to Suzuki Etsu* (Tokyo: Domesu-Shuppan, 1982). Suzuki, an established journalist from the *Asahi* newspaper, became involved with the well-known writer Tamura Toshiko, left his job and arrived in Vancouver in 1918 on the invitation of the community newspaper *Tairiku-Nippo*. Suzuki led the labour union and the daily newspaper *Minshu* and exerted great influence on Japanese Canadian society. He returned to Japan in 1932 and died there one year later.

10. Labour Weekly

11. *Minshu* was first established in 1924 when the number of union members was around 600. Rival newspapers were the *Tairiku Nippo* and *Kanada Nichinichi Shinbun*.

12. Youth associations (or *Seinendan*) were organized on the basis of areas (villages, prefectures, etc.) where people came from. *Isoda* is a *mura* or village composed of three *aza* or hamlets, namely Hassaka, Sugoshi and Mitsuya. *Seinen-dan* thrived along with *Kenjin-kai* (prefectural associations) not only in Canada but in other Japanese enclaves in North and South America.

13. *Taiheiyo Rodosha* translates as Pacific Worker, *Senki*, as Fighting Flag.

14. *Enryo* is an important Japanese concept usually translated as reserve, modesty, and discretion.

15. Morii Etsuji was a gambler who emigrated from Japan in 1906. He became a powerful force in Japanese communities, especially Vancouver, in pre-war British Columbia.

16. Translated as 'Japanese spirit' it became a key word during various pre-war and wartime militaristic campaigns. It refers to the mythic quality of the Japanese psyche. *Yamato* is an ancient name for Japan.

17. A traditional form of Japanese measurement, one *go* equals 180 ml.

18. A special dish of rice and red beans traditionally cooked for celebrations.

19. A chant popular among the Jodo school of Buddhism.

20. The author's cousin H. was born in Canada but was taken to Japan soon after his birth. H. was born at home assisted by midwives and had no birth certificate. The author hired a lawyer in Vancouver and was able to obtain Canadian citizenship for H.

21. Loyalty to the emperor, love of country.

22. *Tanomoshi-ko* is a privately organized mutual financial association, much like a credit union, from which members could borrow money. Since meetings were often held in a party-like atmosphere, the association had an important social function. The associations were very popular in farming communities in Japan and in overseas Japanese immigrant communities.

Selected Bibliography

Adachi, Ken. *The Enemy That Never Was: A History of the Japanese Canadians.* Toronto: McClelland and Stewart, 1976.

Broadfoot, Barry. *Years of Sorrow, Years of Shame: The Story of the Japanese in World War II.* Toronto: Doubleday Canada, 1977.

Ichioka, Yuji. *The Issei: The World of the First Generation Japanese Immigrants, 1885-1924.* New York: The Free Press, 1988.

Kitagawa, Muriel. Ed. Roy Miki. *This is My Own: Letters to Wes and Other Writings on Japanese Canadians, 1941-1948.* Vancouver: Talonbooks, 1985.

Kobayashi, Audrey. *A Demographic Profile of Japanese Canadians and Social Implications for the Future.* Ottawa: Secretary of State, 1989.

Kogawa, Joy. *A Choice of Dreams.* Toronto: McClelland and Stewart, 1974.

———. *Obasan.* Toronto: Lester & Orpen Dennys, 1981.

La Violette, Forrest E. *The Canadian Japanese and World War II: A Sociological and Psychological Account.* Toronto: University of Toronto Press, 1948.

Nakano, Ujo Takeo, with Leatrice Nakano. *Within the Barbed Wire Fence.* Toronto: University of Toronto Press, 1980.

Nakayama, Gordon C. *Issei: Stories of Japanese Canadian Pioneers.* Toronto: Britannia Printers Ltd., 1983.

Shinpo, Mitsuru. *Kanada Nihonjin Imin Monogatari.* Tokyo: Tsukiji-shokan, 1986.

Sunahara, Ann Gomer. *The Politics of Racism: The Uprooting of Japanese Canadians During the Second World War.* Toronto: J. Lorimer, 1981.

Takashima, Shizuye. *A Child in the Prison Camp.* Montreal: Tundra, 1971.

OTHER TITLES OF INTEREST FROM VÉHICULE PRESS

An Everyday Miracle: Yiddish Culture in Montreal
Edited by Ira Robinson, Pierre Anctil and Mervin Butovsky

The Passionate Debate: The Social and Political Ideas of Quebec Nationalism 1920-1945
Michael Oliver

Yellow-Wolf & Other Tales of the Saint Lawrence
Philippe-Joseph Aubert de Gaspé
Translated by Jane Brierley

CIV/n: A Literary Magazine of the 50s
Edited by Aileen Collins

Mapping Literature: The Art and Politics of Translation
Edited by David Homel and Sherry Simon

Despite the Odds: Essays on Canadian Women and Science
Edited by Marianne G. Ainley

Swinging in Paradise: The Story of Jazz in Montreal
John Gilmore